RABIES

Anthrax

Antibiotic-resistant
   Bacteria

Avian Flu

Botulism

Campylobacteriosis

Cervical Cancer

Cholera

Ebola

Encephalitis

Escherichia coli
   Infections

Gonorrhea

Hantavirus Pulmonary
   Syndrome

Helicobacter pylori

Hepatitis

Herpes

HIV/AIDS

Infectious Fungi

Influenza

Legionnaires' Disease

Leprosy

Lyme Disease

Lung Cancer

Mad Cow Disease
   (Bovine Spongiform
   Encephalopathy)

Malaria

Meningitis

Mononucleosis

Pelvic Inflammatory
   Disease

Plague

Polio

Prostate Cancer

Rabies

Salmonella

SARS

Smallpox

Staphylococcus aureus
   Infections

Streptococcus
   (Group A)

Syphilis

Toxic Shock Syndrome

Tuberculosis

Tularemia

Typhoid Fever

West Nile Virus

DEADLY DISEASES AND EPIDEMICS

RABIES

Thomas E. Kienzle, Ph.D.

FOUNDING EDITOR
The Late **I. Edward Alcamo**
Distinguished Teaching Professor of Microbiology,
SUNY Farmingdale

FOREWORD BY
David Heymann
World Health Organization

CHELSEA HOUSE
PUBLISHERS
An imprint of Infobase Publishing

Dedicated to Ed Alcamo

Rabies

Chelsea House
An imprint of Infobase Publishing
132 West 31st Street
New York NY 10001

Library of Congress Cataloging-in-Publication Data
Kienzle, Thomas E.
 Rabies / Thomas E. Kienzle ; foreword by David Heymann.
   p. cm. — (Deadly diseases and epidemics)
 Includes bibliographical references and index.
 ISBN 0-7910-9261-5 (hc : alk. paper)
 1. Rabies—Juvenile literature. I. Title. II. Series.
 RA644.R3K54 2006
 614.5'63—dc22   2006010420

Chelsea House books are available at special discounts when purchased in bulk quantities for businesses, associations, institutions, or sales promotions. Please call our Special Sales Department in New York at (212) 967-8800 or (800) 322-8755.

You can find Chelsea House on the World Wide Web at http://www.chelseahouse.com

Series design by Terry Mallon
Cover design by Keith Trego

Printed in the United States of America

IBT EJB 10 9 8 7 6 5 4 3 2

This book is printed on acid-free paper.

Table of Contents

Foreword

In the 1960s, many of the infectious diseases that had terrorized generations were tamed. After a century of advances, the leading killers of Americans both young and old were being prevented with new vaccines or cured with new medicines. The risk of death from pneumonia, tuberculosis (TB), meningitis, influenza, whooping cough, and diphtheria declined dramatically. New vaccines lifted the fear that summer would bring polio, and a global campaign was on the verge of eradicating smallpox worldwide. New pesticides like DDT cleared mosquitoes from homes and fields, thus reducing the incidence of malaria, which was present in the southern United States and which remains a leading killer of children worldwide. New technologies produced safe drinking water and removed the risk of cholera and other water-borne diseases. Science seemed unstoppable. Disease seemed destined to all but disappear.

But the euphoria of the 1960s has evaporated.

The microbes fought back. Those causing diseases like TB and malaria evolved resistance to cheap and effective drugs. The mosquito developed the ability to defuse pesticides. New diseases emerged, including AIDS, Legionnaires', and Lyme disease. And diseases which had not been seen in decades re-emerged, as the hantavirus did in the Navajo Nation in 1993. Technology itself actually created new health risks. The global transportation network, for example, meant that diseases like West Nile virus could spread beyond isolated regions and quickly become global threats. Even modern public health protections sometimes failed, as they did in 1993 in Milwaukee, Wisconsin, resulting in 400,000 cases of the digestive system illness cryptosporidiosis. And, more recently, the threat from smallpox, a disease believed to be completely eradicated, has returned along with other potential bioterrorism weapons such as anthrax.

The lesson is that the fight against infectious diseases will never end.

In our constant struggle against disease, we as individuals have a weapon that does not require vaccines or drugs, and that is the warehouse of knowledge. We learn from the history of science that "modern" beliefs can be wrong. In this series of books, for example, you will learn that diseases like syphilis were once thought to be caused by eating potatoes. The invention of the microscope set science on the right path. There are more positive lessons from history. For example, smallpox was eliminated by vaccinating everyone who had come in contact with an infected person. This "ring" approach to smallpox control is still the preferred method for confronting an outbreak, should the disease be intentionally reintroduced.

At the same time, we are constantly adding new drugs, new vaccines, and new information to the warehouse. Recently, the entire human genome was decoded. So too was the genome of the parasite that causes malaria. Perhaps by looking at the microbe and the victim through the lens of genetics we will be able to discover new ways to fight malaria, which remains the leading killer of children in many countries.

Because of advances in our understanding of such diseases as AIDS, entire new classes of antiretroviral drugs have been developed. But resistance to all these drugs has already been detected, so we know that AIDS drug development must continue.

Education, experimentation, and the discoveries that grow out of them are the best tools to protect health. Opening this book may put you on the path of discovery. I hope so, because new vaccines, new antibiotics, new technologies, and, most importantly, new scientists are needed now more than ever if we are to remain on the winning side of this struggle against microbes.

David Heymann
Executive Director
Communicable Diseases Section
World Health Organization
Geneva, Switzerland

1

Rabies–
A Zoonotic Disease

Rabies, La Rabia (Spanish), La Rage (French), Die Tollwut (German). This single word, spoken in any language anywhere in the world, invokes fearful visions of a rabid dog, foaming at the mouth, ready to attack anything or anyone that crosses its path. The earliest written records describing this disease and the fate of its victims demonstrated that this fear was well justified, since all persons bitten by a "mad dog" before the 17th century had little chance for survival. Sometimes, this fear turned irrational when people, including those only suspected of having rabies, were hunted down by mobs and killed by stoning, strangulation, or suffocation.[1]

A BRIEF HISTORY OF RABIES

Rabies was first described over 4,000 years ago. A reference from the pre-Mosaic Eshnunna Code of Babylon stated that "if a dog is mad and the authorities have brought the fact to the knowledge of its owner; if he does not keep it in and it bites a man and causes his death, then the owner shall pay two-thirds of a mina (40 shekels) of silver. If it bites a slave and causes his death, he shall pay 15 shekels of silver."[2] Chinese scholars warned of the danger of rabid dogs hundreds of years before the birth of Christ. Aristotle (4th century BC) correctly stated that animals can contract rabies from a bite of a rabid dog, but erroneously declared that man did not get this disease.[2]

During the Renaissance, faith came into play in curing rabies as St. Hubert, one of the healing saints of France and Germany, was thought to employ his powers through a ring or key that was heated red-hot and used to cauterize the wounds inflicted by a rabid dog.[3] Also during this time period, there were numerous reports of outbreaks of rabies in wolves, dogs, and foxes in large regions of Europe.

Although rabies was prevalent in the Old World for thousands of years, its appearance in the New World was less certain due to lack of written records prior to the arrival of Europeans.[3] Shortly after the discovery of the Americas, bishop Petrus Martyr-Anglerius recorded this summary of a bizarre incident, "In several places bats not much smaller than turtle doves used to fly at them [Spanish sailors and soldiers] in the early evening with brutal fury and with their venomous bites brought those injured to madness…[and] bats… come in from the marshes on the river and attack our men with deadly bite."[3] This may have been one of the first descriptions of transmission of rabies by vampire bats.

The first recorded incidence of rabies in North America was in Virginia foxes in 1753. Early records also demonstrated its spread northward to New England in the 1780s, and westward throughout the 19th century. George Washington wrote in his diary in 1769, that he had to shoot a "mad dog" that had bitten several of his hounds.[3]

Important research on treating rabies occurred in 1885, when Louis Pasteur grew "street" (**wild type**) virus in laboratory animals and found he could reduce its **virulence,** or its ability to cause disease, in these animals. Using desiccated spinal cords from rabies-infected rabbits, Pasteur developed the first rabies vaccine. The defining moment occurred when he used his vaccine for the first time on a nine-year-old boy, who had been bitten multiple times by a rabid dog. The child, Joseph Meister, received a total of 13 inoculations and survived.[3]

RABIES IS A ZOONOSIS

An ancient disease that may have predated the appearance of man, rabies is caused by a **virus**, a micro-organism smaller than a bacterium, which infects cells of the nervous system, resulting in fatal inflammation of the brain, or **encephalitis,** if not treated. All mammals, including humans, are susceptible to infection with this virus. Rabies is also classified as **zoonotic** since it is a disease of domestic and wild animals that is transmissible to humans. Many organisms, not just viruses, are

BACTERIA CAN ALSO BE ZOONOTIC

Prior to 2001, few people had ever heard of anthrax. One event, however, brought that word into every household in America and changed forever how mail is handled in this country. That year, spores from the bacterium *Bacillus anthracis* (anthrax) were sent in envelopes through U.S. Postal Service facilities, targeting specific people. These attacks, which occurred in several eastern states, contaminated a number of buildings. Five people died and the buildings were subsequently closed for cleanup. Anthrax, like many viral diseases, is also a zoonotic disease. It infects domestic animals such as cows, sheep, or goats as well as many species of wildlife. This pathogen persists in soil for many years as highly resistant spores. Animals become infected as they graze by ingesting spores from contaminated soil. Although uncommon, human infections do occur, but are generally limited to agriculture workers who come into contact with infected animals or animal products. The anthrax spores used in the terrorist attacks of 2001 were different than those found in soil. Production of those spores, fine enough to be spread through the air, was done intentionally using specialized laboratory equipment solely for the purpose of generating widespread fear.

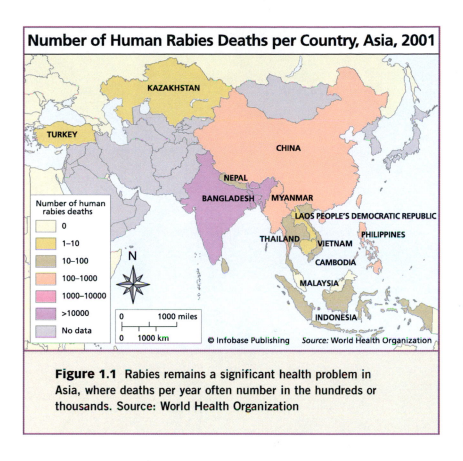

Number of Human Rabies Deaths per Country, Asia, 2001

Number of human rabies deaths

- 0
- 1–10
- 10–100
- 100–1000
- 1000–10000
- >10000
- No data

N

0   1000 miles
0   1000 km

© Infobase Publishing   *Source:* World Health Organization

Figure 1.1 Rabies remains a significant health problem in Asia, where deaths per year often number in the hundreds or thousands. Source: World Health Organization

zoonotic; in the United States alone, there are over 150 known **zoonoses**.

Since the rabies virus is found in saliva, transmission to humans or animals occurs as a result of a bite from a rabid animal. In addition, any contact of saliva with mucous membranes (eyes, nose, mouth) or a wound, such as a cut, can result in transmission of rabies.

ARE YOU SAFE?

Vaccination programs of both humans and domestic animals (dogs and cats) have significantly reduced the incidence of rabies in the United States. As a result, the main animal **reser-**

Figure 1.2 A young boy and his dog look on as people receive food aid from the World Food Program in Zimbabwe. © AP Photo / Karel Prinsloo

voir, where the virus replicates and persists, in this country has switched from dogs to wild animals (raccoons, foxes, skunks, bats, and coyotes). The situation is quite different, however, in many developing countries, where the major rabies reservoir remains unvaccinated domestic dogs and the primary route of transmission is the bites of rabid dogs. Despite intensive research and control efforts, rabies and many other infectious diseases continue to be public health problems.[4] In the United States, for example, between January 1990 and September 2004, there were 44 reported cases of human rabies, with only one to two fatalities per year.[5] In contrast, the World Health Organization (WHO) reports millions of people treated for exposure to rabies each year, and 55,000 human deaths.[6] The majority of these deaths occur in Africa and Asia (Figure 1.2), mostly in children younger than 15 years of age (Figure 1.2). In addition, the cost of treatment following exposure to rabies is prohibitive in many countries where rabies is **endemic** (constantly present to some degree).

2

Nuts and Bolts of Rabies Virus Biology

Viruses are a very diverse group of organisms. The genomes of viruses are either **DNA** or **RNA (molecules that contain genetic information)**, but never both. Some have single-stranded DNA while others have double-stranded DNA. Likewise, RNA viruses can contain single-stranded or double-stranded RNA. Some RNA viruses have segmented genomes. Some viruses are covered in a protein coat, while others have an additional external envelope. By virus standards, there are large viruses and very small viruses, and they come in a wide variety of shapes (Figure 2.1). Consider the information in Table 2.1, to compare the size of humans to that of viruses.

CLASSIFICATION

The rabies virus belongs to the *Rhabdoviridae* family of viruses, a large family of viruses that has widespread distribution in nature, where they infect vertebrates and invertebrates[7], as well as some plants.[8] The rabies virus is categorized with the genus *Lyssavirus* (from Greek meaning "frenzy"). Several additional viruses, such as Lagos bat virus, mokola virus, and duvenhage virus, have also been classified as members of this genus. A second group of viruses within Rhabdoviridae known to infect mammals belongs to the *Vesiculovirus* genus. The most notable virus from this group is the vesicular stomatitis virus, which causes blister-like vesicular lesions

Figure 2.1 (right) Viruses exist in a wide range of sizes, structures, and types. The representations here are drawn to scale. Rabies belongs to the family *Rhabdoviridae*.

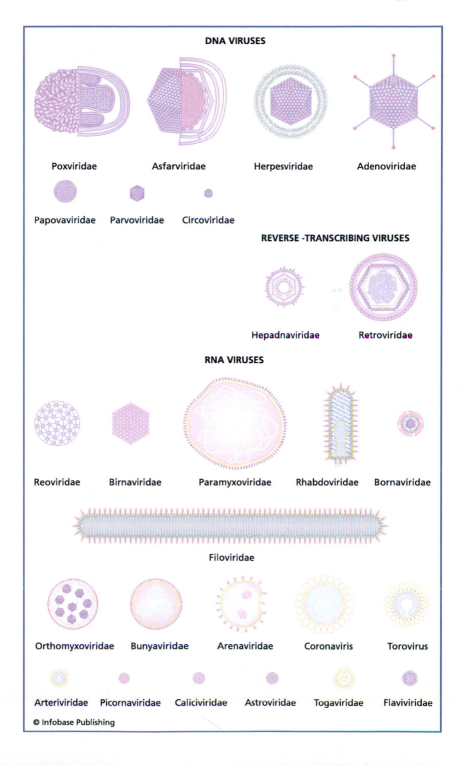

DNA VIRUSES

Poxviridae   Asfarviridae   Herpesviridae   Adenoviridae

Papovaviridae   Parvoviridae   Circoviridae

REVERSE -TRANSCRIBING VIRUSES

Hepadnaviridae   Retroviridae

RNA VIRUSES

Reoviridae   Birnaviridae   Paramyxoviridae   Rhabdoviridae   Bornaviridae

Filoviridae

Orthomyxoviridae   Bunyaviridae   Arenaviridae   Coronaviris   Torovirus

Arteriviridae   Picornaviridae   Caliciviridae   Astroviridae   Togaviridae   Flaviviridae

© Infobase Publishing

on the tongue, gums, teats, and hooves of cattle, horses, and swine.[9] Vesicular stomatitis is one of several viruses that causes a disease indistinguishable from that of foot-and-mouth virus in cattle, which had a devastating economical impact in England during the outbreak of 2001.[10]

STRUCTURE

Rabies virus morphology, or shape, is similar to other family members. It's a bullet-shaped cylinder, rounded on one end and flattened on the other end (Figure 2.2). **Virions**, the infectious offspring of the virus, range in length from 100 to 430 nm

ARE VIRUSES ALIVE?

You may think this is an odd question, but when all the facts are considered, you will see that it does not have a straightforward answer. Let's look first at the arguments against viruses being living organisms.

Viruses are not cells. Even the simplest unicellular microorganisms, such as bacteria, are considered cells since they have their own intracellular machinery for meeting energy requirements and synthesizing macromolecules, thus allowing them to grow. Viruses, on the other hand, are unable to perform any of these essential functions—they lack functional organelles, have no metabolism of their own, and are completely dependent upon living cells to provide them with the metabolic machinery and biochemical energy needed for replication. Outside of host cells, viruses are metabolically inert or inactive.

Many scientists who have spent their careers studying viruses would take the opposite view and consider viruses not only to be alive, but to also have a life as dynamic and complex as any other life forms. While viruses are totally dependent upon the host cells' energy-generating and synthetic (nanometers) and 45 to 100 nm in diameter. Animal rhab-doviruses are usually 180 nm or less, while those that infect plants are typically longer.[11] The center of the rabies virion is made of the single-stranded, genomic RNA, which is tightly bound by the nucleocapsid (N) protein. Together, the N pro-tein/RNA combination makes up the **ribonucleoprotein complex** (RNP), which assumes a helical shape inside the virus particle. Also associated with the RNP are two other proteins, the large (L) protein and the phosophoprotein (P). Surround-ing the RNP is an envelope made up of host-cell lipids within which resides the membrane glycoprotein (G). The "glyco" part

apparatus, their interaction inside of living cells results in a precisely regulated sequence of reactions leading to success-ful reproduction of their own kind. These interactions are dif-ferent for each virus and are of a very complex nature—best understood at the molecular level. By definition, because of their complete dependence on living cells, viruses are consid-ered obligate intracellular parasites. It is interesting to note that certain bacteria, such as members of the genera *Rick-ettsia* and *Chlamydia*, are also obligate intracellular parasites and both are considered life forms.

Your mission, should you choose to accept it, is to research this topic, "The Definition Of Life," which was inten-tionally not covered in the above paragraphs. This will provide you with additional information you can use to develop your own opinion on whether or not you think viruses are alive. As a hint, you may want to first define "life," then ask yourself if this definition is outdated, especially in light of advances being made in science today. Is the definition too narrow? Does it need to be updated? You decide, but remember, be prepared to defend your view!

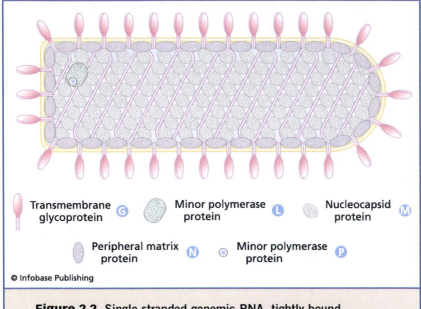

Transmembrane glycoprotein (G)

Minor polymerase protein (L)

Nucleocapsid protein (M)

Peripheral matrix protein (N)

Minor polymerase protein (P)

© Infobase Publishing

Figure 2.2 Single-stranded genomic RNA, tightly bound within the nucleocapsid (N) protein, forms the center of the rabies virion. The N protein N protein/RNA combination, or ribonucleoprotein complex (RNP), takes a helical shape inside the virus particle, where they are surrounded by an envelope of host-cell lipids which contains the membrane glycoprotein (G). The G proteins, which extend outward, also cross the envelope to interact with the matrix (M) protein, which lines the inner wall of the envelope Also associated with the RNP are two other proteins, the large (L) protein and the phosophoprotein (P).

of the name indicates that G is modified during synthesis by the addition of carbohydrate molecules to specific spots on the protein. The G proteins not only extend outward from the surface, but also cross the envelope and interact with the matrix (M) protein, which lines the inner wall of the envelope (Figure 2.2).

GENOME

The genome or genetic material of the rabies virus consists of a continuous nonsegmented strand of RNA, 11,932

Table 2.1 Size Comparison of Viruses, Bacteria, and Other Organisms

10^0	1 m	1m	Human adult males are about 2 meters tall
10^{-1}	0.1m		Human adult hand is about 10 cm wide
10^{-2}	0.01m	1cm	*Aedes aegypti*, adult mosquito is about 1 cm long
10^{-3}	0.001m	1mm	*Ixodes scapularis*, tick, nymphal stage, is about 1mm long
10^{-4}	0.0001m	100µm	Smallest things visible to the naked eye
10^{-5}	0.00001m	10µm	Lymphocytes are about 20µm in diameter Bacillus anthracis, among the largest of pathogenic bacteria is 1?m wide and 5-10µm long
10^{-6}	0.000001m	1µm	Smallest things visible in light microscope are about 0.3µm in size Poxviruses, the largest of the viruses of vertebrates, are 300 nm (or 0.31µm) in their longest dimension
10^{-7}	0.00000001m	100nm	Influenza viruses and retroviruses, typical medium-sized viruses, are about 100 nm in diameter Pestiviruses, such as bovine viral diarrhea virus, typical smaller-sized viruses are about 50 nm in diameter
10^{-8}	0.000000001m	10nm	Picornaviruses, such as foot-and-mouth disease viruses, typical small viruses, are about 30 nm in diameter Circoviruses, the smallest virus of vertebrates, are 17-22 nm in diameter
10^{-9}	0.0000000001m	1nm	Smallest thing visible in transmission electron microscope; DNA double helix diameter is 2 nm
10^{-10}	0.00000000001m	1Å	Diameter of atoms is about 2-3Å

m=meter; cm=centimeter; µm=micrometer; nm=nanometer; Å=Angstrom

Reprinted from *Veterinary Virology* Frederick A. Murphy, Paul J. Gibbs, Marian C. Horzinek, and Michael J. Studdert, eds., "Table 1.2—Perspective on the size of Viruses," page 8, copyright 1999, with permission from Elsevier.

nucleotides in length.[12] The RNA contains five genes designated as N, NS or P, M, G, and L (Figure 2.2 bottom). All of the
viral proteins are synthesized from these genes. Within the
virion, interaction of the matrix protein with the RNP imparts
a tightly coiled configuration to yield the characteristic bullet
shape of the rabies virus.

FUNCTIONS OF PROTEINS

The N or nucleocapsid protein binds to the RNA and is
involved in the important function of tightly packaging the
RNA into the virion. The genomic RNA and N form a complex
that interacts with the P and L proteins for synthesis of new
strands of RNA. In addition, by covering the RNA, N also pro-
tects it from degradation.

The L (large protein) is the viral RNA-dependent RNA
polymerase, which simply means it makes more RNA mole-

A FUN EXERCISE

Here is an exercise that may help you to gain a better understanding of just how small viruses really are. Let's calculate
how many rabies virus particles would fit across the head of a
pin. For this exercise, assume the diameter of a pinhead to be
1.8 mm (millimeters) and the average length of a rabies virion
to be 150 nm (nanometers). This information, plus the data
presented in Table 2.1, gives you all of the necessary figures
needed to solve this problem (remember, you are working in
the metric system and will need to set up conversions). The
solution appears at the end of this chapter. But wait!

Try to figure it out for yourself first. Once you have it figured out, try it again using the sizes given for other viruses in
Table 2.1 to see how many would fit across other objects,
such as your favorite DVD or your fingernail or anything else
that comes to mind.

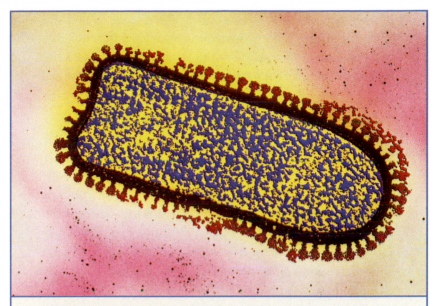

Figure 2.3 Illustration of a rabies virus magnified 100,000 times. © Chris Bjornberg/Photo Researchers, Inc.

cules for packaging into newly formed virions. Within the virion, the L complexes with P, N, and the genomic RNA. This protein is multifunctional and is involved in all major replication steps.

The P or phosphoprotein (also designated as NS) interacts with the L protein and serves to regulate L protein activity. Three molecules of P bind to the RNA, L protein, and N to form a **polymerase,** an active complex that is capable of synthesizing new genomic RNA.

The smallest and most abundant protein found in mature virions is the M or matrix protein. Like L, it too is multifunctional and plays a role in packaging the RNP into new virus particles, adheres to the inner wall of the envelope, interacts with the RNP, and also plays a role in wrapping the host cell membrane around the newly formed virus particles to form the viral envelope.

All rhabdoviruses have proteins on their surface that form spikes. These are G or glycoproteins and are the only viral proteins exposed to the outside world. While part of G spans the envelope to interact with the matrix protein, the majority of the G protein extends beyond the viral membrane. G proteins exist in the envelope as functional, stable **trimers**, proteins with three component parts, to form a coating over the virus particles. The main function of G is to bind protein **receptors** that exist on the surface of host cells. This situation is reminiscent of a lock-and-key: the cellular receptor is the lock and the G protein is the key that "opens" the host cell to provide entry for the virus particle. In fact, binding to a cellular receptor is the first step in the replication process whereby new virus particles are ultimately formed. It is the binding of G to specific receptors on host cells that determines which cells will be infected—not all cells have the same receptors on their surfaces.

REPLICATION STRATEGY

The infection process takes place in several steps or stages as depicted in Figure 2.4. While many of these steps occur simultaneously, it is convenient to consider them as a linear series of events: adsorption, penetration and uncoating, transcription and translation, replication, assembly, and budding.

Infection is initiated by the binding of the viral G protein to its receptor on the surface of host cells. This binding, however, does not occur with just any cellular protein but is restricted to only those proteins G can recognize and attach to. This is called **adsorption** and means that the virion binds to the surface of the host cell. To date, three cellular receptors have been identified that serve as rabies virus receptors. They are the nicotinic acetylcholine receptor,[13] the neural cell adhesion molecule.[14] and the low-affinity nerve-growth factor receptor.[15] In all likelihood, there are more host receptors yet to be identified since the rabies virus has such a broad **host range** (ability to infect many different species).

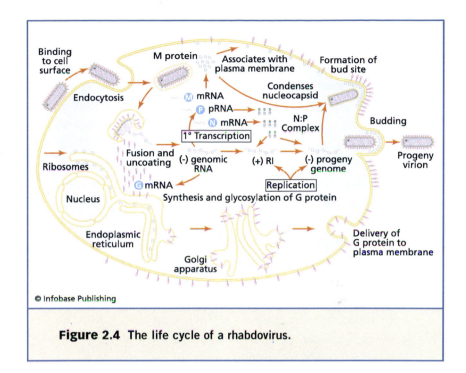

Figure 2.4 The life cycle of a rhabdovirus.

Following contact with cellular receptors, virions enter or penetrate cells through a process called receptor-mediated **endocytosis**. This refers to the formation of a membrane-covered vesicle surrounding the virions. A drop in pH within the vesicle compartment results in a fusion event between the envelope of the virus and the membrane of the vesicle. For rabies, fusion is catalyzed by the G protein and leads to the release of the RNP complex into the cytoplasm of the host cell. Either immediately following membrane fusion or at the same time as fusion, the M protein dissociates from the RNP. It is not clear exactly when this step occurs, and it is not known what triggers the release of M from the RNP.[16] These latter two events, fusion and dissociation of M, constitute the uncoating step of the rabies replication cycle.

Uncoating is immediately followed by **transcription** of rabies-specific **mRNA**s or transcripts by the L protein/P protein complex. Only L has polymerase activity. P serves as an accessory protein and regulates the activity of L by controlling the level of L protein modification with phosphate groups called **phosphorylation**, which is the transfer of a phosphate group from a donor molecule to the L protein. In addition, P itself is also phosphorylated—three molecules of phosphorylated P bind to one molecule of L to form an active polymerase. These modifications are essential for polymerase activity. Transcription begins at the 3' (pronounced "3 prime") end of the genome where the polymerase synthesizes a 50-nucleotide leader. This leader sequence appears on the 5' end ("5 prime") of all viral mRNAs and contains regulatory signals that facilitate translation of the transcripts into proteins. Each of the five mRNAs, encoding the five viral proteins, is then transcribed in the order they appear from the 3' end of the genome. Rabies mRNAs code for only one protein. Some viral mRNAs, such as adenovirus transcripts, code for more than one protein. The number of transcripts (mRNAs) made for each protein forms a gradient from the 3' end, so that N protein transcripts are the most abundant while L protein transcripts are the least abundant. This phenomenon is regulated in part by nucleotides present between each viral gene at which the polymerase pauses when it finishes making one transcript. It then has to re-initiate transcription at the beginning of the next gene. This mechanism constitutes a stop-and-start model of transcription.

Once mRNAs are synthesized, **translation** begins on free cellular **ribosomes,** an organelle present in the cytoplasm. Translation is simply taking the information present in the transcript and converting it into proteins. While the translation of the G protein begins on free ribosomes, its synthesis is completed in another cytoplasmic organelle, the **endoplasmic reticulum,** where it receives carbohydrate modifications before being incorporated into the host cell membrane. M protein accumulates in patches on the inside of the cell

SOLUTION TO PROBLEM PRESENTED IN FACT BOX 2.2

First, write down what we know:

  1.8mm = diameter of pin head

  150nm = length of rabies virus

Second, set up conversions so that we are working with the same units by changing our known values to either mm or to nm. Let's convert everything to mm.

$$150nm \quad \times \quad \frac{1\mu m}{1,000nm} \quad \times \quad \frac{1mm}{1,000\mu m} \quad =$$

Third, to make this conversion, cancel out like units and do the multiplication. When you do this, you end up with the desired units of measure, mm.

$$150\cancel{nm} \quad \times \quad \frac{1\cancel{\mu m}}{1,000\cancel{nm}} \quad \times \quad \frac{1mm}{1,000\cancel{\mu m}} \quad = \quad \frac{150mm}{1,000,000}$$

Fourth, do the division.

$$\frac{150mm}{1,000,000} \quad = \quad 0.00015mm$$

This says that 150nm are equal to 0.00015 mm. Since we have now converted the nm to mm, we are ready to solve the problem.

Fifth, set up the equation as follows (remember to cancel out the units).

$$\frac{1.8\cancel{mm}}{0.00015\cancel{mm}} \quad = \quad 12,000$$

  It would take 12,000 rabies virus particles, laid end to end, to reach across the head of a pin. Now that's small!

membrane. These regions are where budding will eventually occur.

Accumulation of M protein triggers the switch from transcription to **replication** (process of duplication) of new genomic RNA molecules. The signals involved in this switch are complex but also involve N binding to the 50 nucleotide leader, the phosphorylation state of N, continued translation of viral proteins, and a modification of P protein that alters its activity. With N protein present, P is no longer modified by phosphorylation and as a result, P interacts not only with L, but also with N to form a P-L-N complex (if you recall, three molecules of P complexed with one L to form a polymerase, but now one P interacts with one N and one L). This new complex, called a replicase, makes new genomic RNA that will become part of new virions.[17]

As the nascent genomic RNA is being formed, the P-L-N complex encapsidates or binds it to form new RNP complexes. This is the first step in the **assembly** process that makes new virions. The encapsidated RNP migrates to the host cell membrane, particularly to regions enriched in M and G proteins. As the RNP associates with the cell membrane, M initiates **condensation**, or packaging, of the RNP into the characteristic coiled shape.[18]

Once condensation begins, **budding** is initiated from the host cell membrane. This is the final step of maturation of rabies virus replication and results in the release of newly formed virions. As the virions bud, they are enclosed by part of the host cell membrane. No longer associated with the cell, newly formed viruses are now capable of infecting other host cells (or a different host) to initiate the replication cycle all over again.

3

Pathogenesis of Rabies

Because millions of signals are traveling through your nervous system, you are able to read these words. At the same time, other signals maintain your posture, digest the food you ate at your last meal, and keep your body warm. Little wonder then, that the human nervous system is a biologically privileged site—nerve fibers are wrapped in a special myelin coat to provide nourishment, only certain molecules are allowed to enter the central nervous system (**CNS**), protected by what is known as the **blood-brain barrier** that limits movement of molecules into the brain; and the brain has an extensive blood supply that maximizes the amount of oxygen and blood it receives.

You may think that being so special, the CNS would be completely protected from pathogens, but that is not the case. In fact, several viruses have a predilection for the central nervous system. Overall, however, viral infections of the CNS are infrequent and usually result in a self-limited infection. Despite this, CNS tissue is highly susceptible to damage with slow or incomplete recovery, so infections to this area of the body take on enhanced importance because of the potential for death or permanent impairment.

Rabies virus is one of the viruses that has an affinity for cells of the nervous system. Once it reaches the CNS, there is rapid replication with eventual onset of disease. Although the disease may not be exactly the same for each person, rabies in humans has been divided into five general stages (Table 3.1): incubation, **prodrome** of nonspecific symptoms, acute neurologic syndrome, coma, and death.[19]

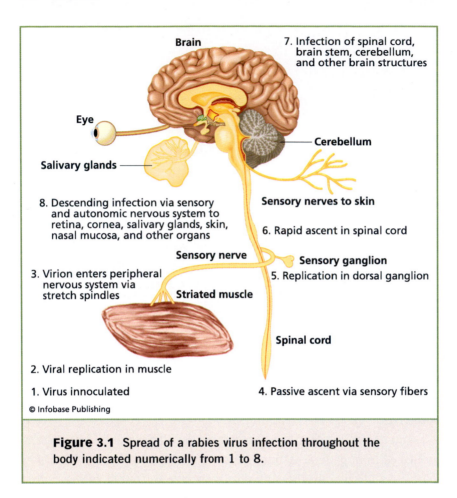

Brain

7. Infection of spinal cord, brain stem, cerebellum, and other brain structures

Eye

Cerebellum

Salivary glands

Sensory nerves to skin

8. Descending infection via sensory and autonomic nervous system to retina, cornea, salivary glands, skin, nasal mucosa, and other organs

6. Rapid ascent in spinal cord

Sensory nerve

Sensory ganglion

3. Virion enters peripheral nervous system via stretch spindles

5. Replication in dorsal ganglion

Striated muscle

Spinal cord

2. Viral replication in muscle

1. Virus innoculated

4. Passive ascent via sensory fibers

© Infobase Publishing

Figure 3.1 Spread of a rabies virus infection throughout the body indicated numerically from 1 to 8.

In 1546, Italian physician Girolamo Fracastoro provided a graphic description of the inevitable course of clinical rabies. Following a bite from a rabid animal, its "incubation is so stealthy, slow and gradual that the infection is very rarely manifest before the 20th day, in most cases after the 30th, and in many cases not until four or six months have elapsed." As the disease progressed, "the patient can neither stand nor lie down; like a madman he flings himself hither and thither, tears his flesh with his hands, and feels intolerable thirst. This is the most distressing symptom, for he so shrinks from water and all liquids that he would rather die than drink or be brought near to water; it is then that they bite other persons, foam at the mouth, their eyes look twisted, and finally they are exhausted and painfully breathe their last."[2]

INCUBATION PERIOD

A bite from an infected animal may result in the deposition of rabies-containing saliva into striated muscle and connective

HERPES SIMPLEX VIRUS TYPE I

Although very different from the rabies virus, particularly in terms of size and genetic makeup, some herpes viruses also tend to infect cells of the nervous system. One of the human herpes viruses, herpes simplex virus type 1 (HSV-1), infects the sensory nerves of the face. It is a common pathogen with worldwide distribution. In fact, more than half of your fellow classmates are already infected with this virus right now and don't even know it! That's one of the hallmarks of HSV-1 infections—asymptomatic infections. But the most famous characteristic of HSV-1 is its ability to establish a latent infection in peripheral nerves. Latency refers to a stage of infection when the replication cycle is arrested. During this arrested or latent stage, the virus is not replicating and exhibits only minimal activity. When conditions are right, however, the replication cycle is reinitiated and completed. What are these "conditions"? They include a variety of unrelated environmental and biological triggers, such as stress, menstruation, or too much exposure to sunlight, which can stimulate a new round of active infection (known as a recurrent or reactivated infection). An example of a recurrent HSV-1 infection is the infamous cold sore on the lip or nose that seems to appear at the worst possible time—such as just before an important date!

Table 3.1 The Different Stages of Rabies

Stage	Type	Duration	Associated Findings
Incubation period		Under 30 days	None
			(25%); 30-90 days (50%); 90 days-1 year (20%); over 1 year (5%)
Prodrome and early symptoms		2-10 days	Parasthesias or pain at the wound site, fever, malaise, anorexia, nausea, and vomiting
Acute neurologic	Furious rabies (80%)	2-7 days	Hallucinations, disease, bizarre behavior, anxiety, agitation, biting, hydrophobia, autonomic dysfunction, syndrome of inappropriate antidiuretic hormone (SIADH)
Acute neurologic disease	Paralytic rabies (20%)	2-7 days	Ascending flaccid paralysis
Coma death*		0-14 days	

*Rare recoveries have been reported

Reprinted from *Infections of the Central Nervous System*, W. Michael Scheld, Richard J. Whitley and David T. Durack, eds., copyright 1991, with permission from Lippincott-Raven.

tissue. Less frequently, infection may occur when saliva comes into contact with a skin abrasion or mucous membranes. The virus is not, however, able to penetrate intact skin.

Initially, the virus replicates in muscle cells, which results in an increase in the number of virus particles at the bite site (Figure 3.1). In the United States, most bites from dogs occur on peripheral limbs (legs, arms). The amount of time the rabies virus remains at the initial infection site, called the incubation period, varies considerably but usually averages from one to three months, although the appearance of symptoms

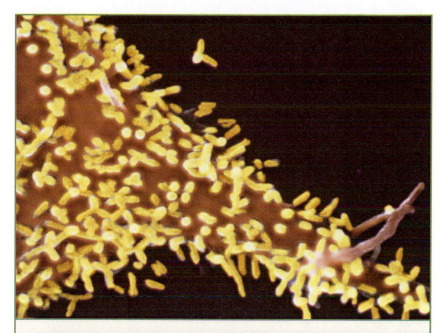

Figure 3.2 Colored scanning electron micrograph of rabies virus particles infecting a mammalian cell. © Dr. Gopal Murti/ Photo Researchers, Inc.

just a few days or even years after exposure has been observed.[20] Exactly why long incubation periods occur is not completely understood, although the virus probably remains in muscle cells during this time. Long incubation periods can be problematic by delaying immediate treatment—particularly if there is no known history of an animal bite (as may occur with bats). Factors that influence the incubation period include size of initial **inoculum** (the amount of virus delivered with the initial bite), extent of nerve supply to the wound, severity of the bite, distance from bite site to the spinal cord, and host age and immune status.

Regardless of the length of the incubation period, the virus eventually infects the nerves present at the area of the wound.

At this point, the rabies virus binds to receptors for neuro-transmitters and gains access to peripheral neurons. It then moves to the spinal cord by **passive transport** along the nerves, which may take several days. In contrast to movement within nerves of the periphery, once the virus reaches the spinal cord, it moves rapidly to the brain and appears to follow the pattern of synaptic connections.[21] Evidence from animal models of rabies suggest this movement may occur in just hours.[22] Clinical evidence of such rapid movement comes from the quick onset of ascending paralysis seen in some human cases. Once in the brain, widespread dissemination occurs, with the virus infecting neurons in multiple regions of the brain (Figure 3.1).

XENOTRANSPLANTATION

Organ transplantation or corneal transplantation from one human to another has saved countless lives or saved numerous peoples' eyesight. Another type of transplantation is relatively new and is known as xenotransplantation. While it still involves organ replacement in humans, the donor is not another human being. The prefix "xeno," which means "foreign" or "other," is a clue that something drastically different is included in these types of procedures.

Xenotransplantation, therefore, is the transplantation of an organ from one species to another—in this case to humans. Currently, the most popular species used for this type of organ replacement is the pig, particularly pigs genetically engineered to carry human genes. Other species of interest for transplantation into humans includes non-human primates and bovine (cows).

While this sounds like cool cutting-edge science, is it really necessary to put animal organs into humans? The answer is a resounding yes, because there is a critical shortage of

PRODROME

The prodrome period lasts three or four days and begins with symptoms including nervousness, anxiety, or other behavioral changes; headaches; fever; nausea; vomiting; chills; **photophobia** (intolerance to light); and local pain at the bite wound. These symptoms are quite general and could be signs of many different viral infections. Making the diagnosis of rabies would be rare at this stage without evidence of an animal bite.

Most virus replication appears to occur in the limbic system of the brain, which is the portion of the brain associated with emotions, and can lead to the altered and aggressive behaviors characteristic of this disease. While there is variation between persons, the symptoms actually exhibited usually

human organs available for those needing transplants. As a result, thousands of people die each year due to this shortage. Just imagine an endless supply of organs or tissues available to meet the ever-growing demand for patients in need. An early famous case, from Loma Linda, California in 1984, involved a heart transplant from a baboon to Baby Fae, who survived for 21 days and made medical history.

While many advances in this technology have been made since, one of the major obstacles that is currently being addressed is the risk of transmission of animal pathogens, such as viruses, to human recipients. To date, use of very sensitive tests has found no evidence for transmission of pig viruses to humans. There is no doubt that further research is needed to solve major hurdles, but preliminary results suggest it is time for a major push forward in research to advance xenotransplantation to the next level of use in humans.

(Source: Fishman, J. A., and C. Patience. "Xenotransplantation: infectious risk revisited." *American Journal of Transplantation* 4 (2004): 1383-1390.)

depend upon which anatomical regions of the brain are infected. A mild infection of the cerebral cortex for example, may allow one to remain alert through the early stages of the disease.

ACUTE NEUROLOGIC SYNDROME

This phase is characterized by the onset of impaired coordination, paralysis, fear of water or air, confusion, hallucinations, hyperactivity, aggressiveness, or aberrant sexual behavior. This stage may last approximately one week.

As the virus continues to replicate and spread within the brain, it travels down peripheral nerves to infect multiple organs of the body, including salivary glands. Rabies virus is able to replicate within salivary glands, resulting in high concentrations of virus. This latter point means that the time when there is the development of aggressive behavior in animals, such as dogs, is the same time when there is the maximum amount of virus in the saliva and, hence, is the best time to bite another host to start the infection cycle over again. Aggressive behavior can also occur in humans, but usually there is limited spread of rabies by human bite.

Human cases of rabies have been divided into two types: furious, and paralytic (dumb) rabies. Patients in whom hyperactivity predominates are classified as having furious rabies. Such cases may exhibit extreme excitability; a soft touch is painful and can lead to violent motor responses and convulsions. The hallmark of rabies, hydrophobia (fear of water), occurs during the furious form and is due to contraction of the throat muscles when swallowing and results in foaming at the mouth. Even the attempt to drink water can trigger a hydrophobic episode, which may last from one to five minutes. In fact, hydrophobia is an ancient term used to describe this disease.

About 20 percent of human cases exhibit paralytic or dumb rabies. These cases seem to occur in persons exposed to rabies virus from certain animals, such as vampire bats.[23] Initially such patients develop pain at the site of the wound and then develop weakness, followed by paralysis, usually in the bitten extremity. Paralysis then progresses to involve all limbs (quadriplegia).

COMA AND DEATH

With furious rabies, patients usually enter a coma after about seven days. This may be delayed in paralytic rabies, with some patients surviving up to a month before progressively declining into coma. The coma stage may last three to seven days. Death is usually sudden and due to cardiac or respiratory failure.

4

Domestic Animals and Wildlife

DOMESTIC ANIMALS AND WILDLIFE

Imagine a friendly, loving pet that suddenly turns vicious or displays other unusual behavior. That is definitely a scary scenario, but one which would not have been surprising in this country more than 50 years ago. Strict animal control and vaccination laws have significantly reduced the possibility of such a scene.

Humans are dead-end or terminal hosts for several viruses, including rabies. This simply means that humans are not required for maintenance of the virus in its normal transmission cycle (i.e., humans are not one of the reservoir hosts). The reason is because the virus cannot reach high-enough levels in the human body to be easily transmitted to another human being or host, although it is possible for rabies to be transmitted via a bite to another human. Rabies is maintained in nature via animals such as foxes, skunks, or raccoons. Some examples of other viruses for which humans are dead-end hosts include Dengue virus, Hantavirus pulmonary syndrome, Hepatitis A virus, and Western encephalitis virus.

DOGS

Rabies in dogs and cats has phases similar to those observed in the course of human rabies. During the two- to three-day prodromal phase, dogs may exhibit nervousness, apprehension, solitude, anxiety, and may display a "far away" look due to dilation of pupils (Figure 4.1). Animals that are usually friendly may suddenly become shy or irritable and have enhanced responses to auditory and visual stimuli. The furious phase

Figure 4.1 A dog suspected of being rabid after exhibiting signs of restlessness and aggressive behavior. Source: Centers for Disease Control and Prevention

may be characterized by restlessness, photophobia, excessive salivation, and roaming, during which time they may bite or eat unusual objects, such as wood. Many owners think their pet has something stuck in its throat due to it making choking sounds; during attempts to remove this object, owners or veterinarians may become exposed to rabies-containing saliva. Dogs may also avoid people and seek dark places to hide. Muscles of the **larynx** or voicebox may become paralyzed with a resulting characteristic high-pitched bark or yowl.[24] They usually exhibit lack of muscle coordination, disorientation, and generalized or **grand mal** seizures—they may die during a seizure episode. Interestingly, despite what is commonly believed about dogs and rabies, they are actually only moderately susceptible to rabies (Table 4.1). The presence of **antibodies,** or blood proteins

Table 7.2 Susceptibility of Various Animal Species to Rabies

Very High	High	Moderate	Low
Cotton rats	Bats	Dogs	Opossums
Coyotes	Cattle	Primates	
Foxes	Domestic Cats		
Jackals	Hamsters		
Kangaroos	Rabbits		
Voles	Raccoons		
Wolves	Skunks		

Source: Bleck, Thomas E. and Charles E. Rupprecht. Chapter 38 in *Clinical Virology*, Douglas D. Richman, Richard J. Whitely, and Frederick G. Hayden, Eds., Washington, D.C.: ASM Press, 2002.

that destroy infectious organisms, to rabies in dogs in endemic areas indicates many survive after being bitten by a rabid animal, thus supporting this classification.[25]

CATS

Most cats exhibit furious rabies, showing erratic or unusual behavior for one or two days, with impaired corneal reflexes and fever. They may also become anxious and have a blank or spooky look in their eyes. During the furious phase, they frequently bite or scratch without provocation. If they are confined to a cage, they may attempt to bite or scratch at moving objects, such as when someone walks past the cage. While cats are less likely to display paralysis of the larynx, owners usually detect an increase in the frequency of vocalization as well as a change in pitch of their pet's call. Cats may exhibit muscular tremors and weakness or run continuously until they collapse and die. Table 4.1 shows that cats' susceptibility to rabies is rated as high.

DOMESTIC ANIMALS

Animals such as horses, cows, and other farm animals that remain outside much of the time are at increased risk of exposure to rabid animals and thus pose an increased threat for public health. The diagnosis of rabies can be difficult due to variable or nonspecific clinical signs. In horses, symptoms may include irregularity of muscle action or paralysis of hindquarters, lying down, pharyngeal paralysis, loss of anal sphincter tone, fever, and an increased sensitivity to sensory stimuli. Once clinical signs become apparent, average survival time is about five days. Supportive treatment has no effect on the course of the disease.[26]

In cows, symptoms include excessive salivation, behavioral change, muzzle tremors, bellowing, aggression, hyperexcitability, and pharyngeal paralysis. The furious form of rabies was found in cattle, observed in 70 percent of those experimentally infected as part of a vaccine testing program.[27] In natural infections, however, paralytic rabies has been observed so frequently that it is referred to by different names in different countries, i.e., *derriengue* ("incoordinated disease") in Mexico and *mal de caderas* ("hip ill") in Argentina.[3]

Obviously, cattle rabies is extremely important in Central and South America. In one outbreak alone, between 1954 and 1968, over 260,000 cattle died in southern Bolivia and northern Argentina.[2]

Interestingly, in Hungary, cattle rabies has become a major problem due to infection not only by rabid wildlife (foxes), but also by rabid cats.[28] This should not be too surprising since, as we learned above, rabid cats can become very aggressive.

WILDLIFE

Rabies in wild animals is usually associated with skunks, raccoons, foxes, bats, coyotes, and mongooses in North America, Europe, South Africa, and some Caribbean islands. The clinical course of rabies in these animals is similar to that described already, although there may be variation for any individual animal. A bite from a rabid animal is followed by an incubation period that usually lasts between two weeks and 90 days, although it may last much longer. A prodromal phase precedes actual onset of disease symptoms, which may take the furious or paralytic form of rabies. The chief characteristic of wild animal rabies is their loss of fear of humans and larger animals, which may lead to episodes of biting objects, other animals, or

A CORRIDO ("FOLKSONG") ABOUT RABIES

In 1963, a rabies outbreak in cattle prompted a rancher from Mexico, Rosendo Reyes, to write a song about the devastating effects rabies can have on peoples' livelihood, particularly on the poorest people whose only income was completely dependent upon their few head of livestock.

A corrido I'm going to sing
Hope nobody gets offended
I only want to tell you, about that "derriengue."
This "derriengue" business, is really quite a thing
Believe me at the rate it's going, we'll be left with less than
  nothing.
With this sad death, you see no money flow
It's already done in the cattle of Ajal and Rincon Vaquero.
The death moves, killing cow and horse, just see it go
Around Almoloya, the Haciendita and the Barrio
When you pass the plum orchard you see the buzzards low,
They're picking away at the cows of Don Waldo Cabrero.
The cows are dying, both calves and old cattle
In the place called Collolapa.
They die straight on, not even the tail's for you,
They're already dying by Paso Falso

people. Therefore, any unprovoked bite from a wild animal should raise concerns for possible rabies infection.

In the United States, several different animals serve as major reservoirs for rabies, depending upon location; for example, raccoons are the predominant species in the northeast while skunks are the prime species in the Midwest. Some skunks may contain the rabies virus in their saliva for up to 18 days before death and are quite aggressive during that period of

And now it's at Chigola.
Two big cows died, the hides couldn't be used, oh no,
One died at Reforma, the other at Sardinero
Look, dear God, you've killed enough it seems,
Gone is Uncle Martiniano Rueda's prize ox team.
And Mr. Angel Dolores, well, he talked to me right
    straight,
With that damned derriengue, ten of his cows met their
    fate.
We're lamenting it now, it's not e'en the exceptions but
    the rule,
It's killed Uncle Pedro's ox, and old Lolo's bull.
Many are complaining, no action, just words again,
What we need is the fame of some great veterinarian.
When they go out to sell the meat,
Man, don't even turn it over,
They say it's "that derriengue"
Who'd eat that now—or ever.
With that I take my leave, but not from this place,
I want a stiff battle against this worldwide plague.

Source: G. M. Baer. "Rabies Virus." In: *Virology*, ed. B.N. Fields. Raven Press, New York, NY: 1985, p. 1147.

Figure 4.2 A caged rabid fox. Source: Centers for Disease Control and Prevention

time, making them very effective at spreading the disease.[2] In Europe, foxes have historically been the reservoir for rabies— rabies has spread 30 kilometers per year from east to west since World War II.[2] In Germany, fox rabies occurs in three-year cycles, with 50 percent of foxes succumbing to the disease in areas where they exist at one or more fox per square kilometer. It is of interest to note, that even this high death rate is not sufficient to eliminate rabies completely; in Denmark, rabies disappears spontaneously only when the fox population is reduced to one animal per four or five square kilometers.[2]

5

Epidemiology

Not all rabies viruses are exactly the same, genetically speaking. This is also true for other viruses, such as West Nile virus or Ebola virus. In fact, this is true of all viruses. Interestingly, this is also true for most living things on this planet, including humans. Imagine a planet where every person had exactly the same genetic makeup—everyone would look the same, act the same, talk the same, and even smell the same as everyone else. How boring! Thanks to variations in our genetic makeup, that is not the case. Scientists are now able, with the completion of the Human Genome Project, to relate these variations or genetic changes to specific diseases.

Such changes are also found in viruses and lead to the definition of virus variants. Every virus undergoes genetic changes in its genomic sequence (i.e., **mutations**) every time it replicates inside a host. Mutations are especially prevalent in RNA viruses as compared to DNA viruses due to a higher rate of "mistakes" or mutations during the replication process.

For rabies virus, specific genetic changes have been found that always occur within a particular host; for example, there is a specific set of changes in the rabies virus found in bats and only in bats. The same is true for dogs, foxes, skunks, and other wildlife reservoirs of this virus. Thus we have bat variants of the rabies virus, canine variants, raccoon variants, and so on. Hence, when a person is diagnosed with rabies, it is possible, from the sequence of the virus genome, to determine from which animal that person contracted rabies.

UNITED STATES

In the United States, there is little fear of getting sick from drinking contaminated water; there is easy access to medical care, and vaccination programs in early childhood to ward off diseases. Large-scale animal vaccination programs for rabies are another example. Implementation of strict vaccination and leash laws during the 1940s and 1950s significantly reduced the number of human rabies cases due to rabid dogs and has all but eliminated the canine variant from circulation (Figure 5.1). When a canine variant emerged in coyotes in south Texas during the '70s and '80s, control programs, such as prohibiting movement of wild animals for purposes of hunting or restocking, were successfully initiated to interrupt the spread of rabies and to prevent the accidental introduction of rabies into unaffected areas.[32]

TOOLS OF THE EPIDEMIOLOGIST

Simply put, epidemiology is the study of the factors (cause, distribution, dynamics, and transmission) involved in diseases in specific populations. Epidemiologists may use such tools as virologic, serologic, molecular, and ecologic markers, and computer-assisted data and modeling. These tools provide epidemiologists with data on diseases that they evaluate to determine rates of mortality, seasonal variations of disease, and geographic distributions of disease in regions of the country. Electron microscopy would be an example of a virologic technique in which viruses can be identified by their characteristic morphology. Determining the number of people who have serum antibodies to a virus was a serologic tool used by early virologist to map the worldwide distribution of exposure to yellow fever virus during the 1930s.[29] The latest molecular techniques available today allow scientists to compare the nucleic acid sequences (DNA or RNA) of viruses and, thus, to establish how closely related virus strains are that have caused multiple outbreaks (e.g.,

One result of regulations directed at companion animals and education programs designed to help eliminate rabies from specific areas is that today in the United States, the vast majority of rabies cases are confined to wild animals (Figure 5.2). Additional programs directed at safeguarding domestic livestock, vaccination of wildlife, as well as continued regulations concerning confinement of pets, have together reduced the number of transmission incidents to humans.

Within the last several years, however, there have been an increasing number of human rabies cases involving bat variants of the rabies virus.[33] In many cases, there is no history of a bite from a bat—likely due to a bite that went unnoticed or

Norovirus outbreaks on cruise ships during 2002-2003).[30] Ecologic techniques would include not only how a virus interacts with its host, but also how this interaction is altered by human intrusion into new environments, such as invasion into and destruction of rain forests and the emergence of new viral diseases (e.g., Ebola). Finally, the latest in computer software allows scientists to develop models of how a virus might be spread under specific weather or atmospheric conditions. An example of this technique was the development of models for the spread of foot-and-mouth disease virus by wind based on the outbreak of this virus in England in 2001.[31] The goal of such models is to identify high-risk regions or areas with a high density of livestock and to simulate the impact an outbreak may have in a particular locale. These models allow for quicker responses to avoid the economic devastation the foot-and-mouth disease virus outbreak had on the cattle industry in the United Kingdom.

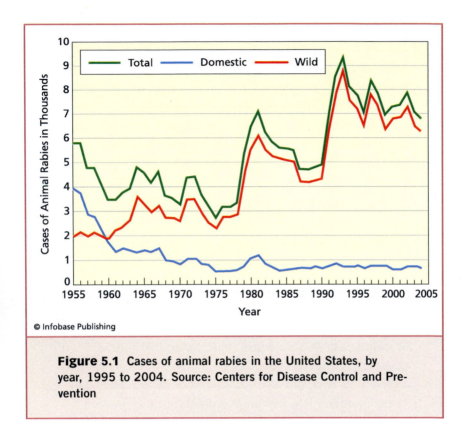

© Infobase Publishing

Figure 5.1 Cases of animal rabies in the United States, by year, 1995 to 2004. Source: Centers for Disease Control and Prevention

forgetting about an encounter with a bat because it was considered insignificant.

Rabies cases of wildlife in the United States occur in geographically defined regions (Figure 5.3) where transmission occurs within members of the same species. That said, however, **spillover** (the occurrence of one variant of rabies in a different species) does occur but usually without establishment of a new variant in that region. If a rabies variant is successfully transmitted in a new region, it can become established in a species for centuries, becoming **enzootic** in that animal population. The boundaries shown in Figure 5.3 should only be considered estimations and may expand or contract through virus

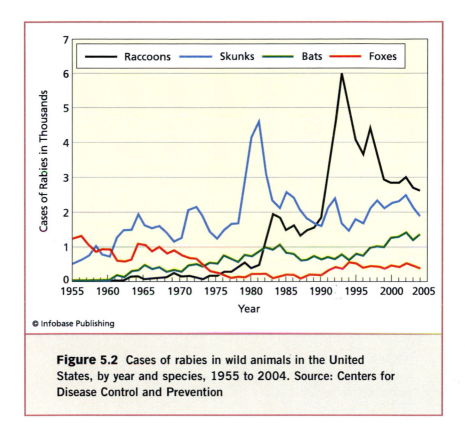

Figure 5.2 Cases of rabies in wild animals in the United States, by year and species, 1955 to 2004. Source: Centers for Disease Control and Prevention

transmission or interaction of populations of animals. One way for this to occur is for the population of an animal species to increase, resulting in higher population densities in one area and emigration to other areas and thus an expansion of the boundary for a particular variant. Natural obstacles to animal movement, such as mountains or large bodies of water, may help in maintaining lower population densities and therefore slow the spread of rabies.

Reports on rabies are performed each year to inform veterinarians and public health officials of its current status, geographic distribution, and short-term and long-term patterns for certain animal species. Long-term reports examine data

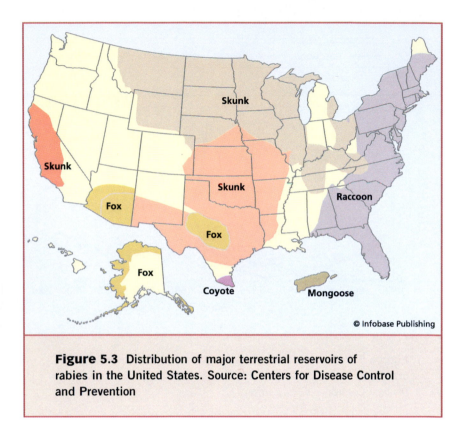

Figure 5.3 Distribution of major terrestrial reservoirs of rabies in the United States. Source: Centers for Disease Control and Prevention

from 1955 and yield trends of cases of rabies in animals. Short-term reports are done by comparing results of the current years' reports to those from the previous year (e.g., 2003 compared to 2002) and by examining seasonal patterns for specific species of animals. Summaries of such reports are provided to Mexico and Canada due to common borders and the high number of travelers between these two countries and the United States. Data for the annual reports come from each state reporting the number of rabies cases, county of origin, and type of animal to the Centers for Disease Control and Prevention each month. Year-end totals are confirmed by telephone verification with state or territorial health departments.

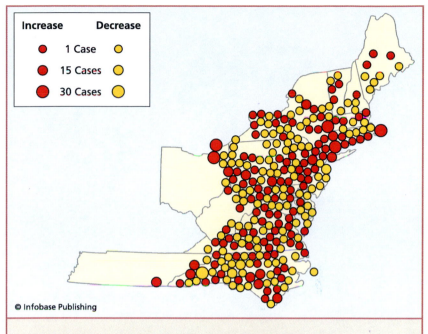

Figure 5.4 Changes in cases of rabies in raccoons in the mid-Atlantic and northeastern states, 2003 to 2004. Dot size is proportional to the number of cases in the country. Source: Centers for Disease Control and Prevention

WILD ANIMALS

Rabies in wild animals accounted for more than 90 percent of the total number of cases reported in 2003. This number is 11.1 percent less than the total number of cases (7,375) reported for 2002. Raccoons were the most commonly reported rabid animal in 2003, followed by skunks, bats, and foxes.

The number of raccoon rabies reported in 2003 (2,635) represents a five-year low (Figure 5.4) and includes 10 of the 20 eastern states where raccoon rabies has become enzootic. There were several cases of raccoon rabies reported in Texas, but these represented spillover rabies from other species, such as from the gray fox.

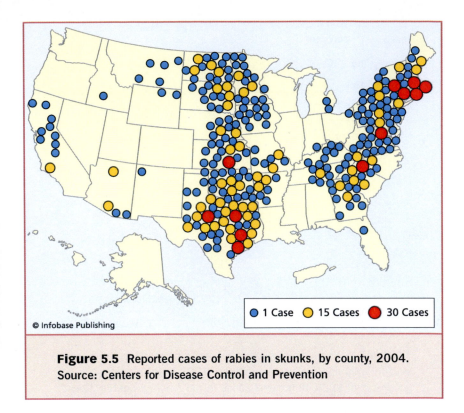

Figure 5.5 Reported cases of rabies in skunks, by county, 2004. Source: Centers for Disease Control and Prevention

Unnatural movement of animals can quickly introduce rabies into new areas; such events are usually initiated by humans. An example includes the inadvertent translocation of rabies-infected raccoons from an old endemic area in Florida to West Virginia in 1977.[34] Since some raccoons were infected with rabies, this movement initiated an **epizootic**, an outbreak of disease in an animal population, in this region of the country. Before, there had been separate foci of raccoon rabies populations in the southeast and mid-Atlantic States. Now, however, these foci have merged with raccoon rabies enzootic in all states along the eastern coast as well as Alabama, Ohio, Pennsylvania, Vermont, and West Virginia.

Three skunk variants (i.e., three separate foci of skunk rabies) exist in California and the north central and south central states (Figure 5.5). The states where raccoon rabies is enzootic reported 38.7 percent of the total number of skunk rabies for 2003 (Figure 5.5), presumably due to spillover from rabies-infected raccoons.

A very old reservoir of fox rabies exists in red and arctic foxes in Alaska. Rabies-infected foxes spread across Canada and into some of the New England states during the 1950s. While fox rabies is enzootic in Alaska, its numbers are decreasing in Canada. Most of the cases of rabid foxes in 2003 were from the states that are currently enzootic for raccoon rabies and, like skunk rabies in this region, probably represents spillover transmission.

Bat rabies is unique in that transmission appears to be **intraspecific** (i.e., within species), which has resulted in the development of distinct variants associated with different bat species. In addition, due to greater mobility of bats, as compared to terrestrial animals, it is not possible to develop range maps for the different variants. Since bat species known to be reservoirs for rabies exist in all states except Hawaii, each state is considered enzootic for bat rabies (Figure 5.6). In 2003, 16.9 percent of all rabies cases were due to bat rabies (1,212 cases), which is a decline of 11.7 percent compared to 2002. This is the first decrease in bat rabies since the year 2000. Many of the reports indicating rabies in bats were not able to identify the bat to the taxonomic level of species (most were identified to the taxonomic level of order only). Of those that were identified to the species level, 46.5 percent were the big brown bat (*Eptesicus fuscus*), 27.4 percent the Brazilian (Mexican) free-tailed bat (*Tadarida brasiliensis*), 5.8 percent the hoary bat (*Lasiurus cinereus*), 3.2 percent the Seminole bat (*Lasiurus seminolus*), 1.7 percent the silver-haired bat (*Lasionycteris noctivagans*), and 0.8 percent were the eastern pipistrelle (*Pipistrellus subflavus*), just to name some of the bats reported in 2003.[35]

An interesting observation has been noted in relation to rabies variants of bats and bat-associated rabies in humans.

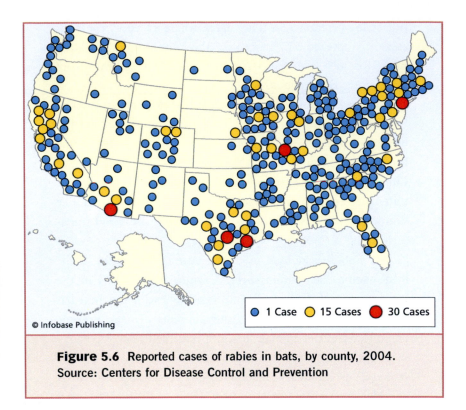

Figure 5.6 Reported cases of rabies in bats, by county, 2004.
Source: Centers for Disease Control and Prevention

Two species of bats, the eastern pipistrelle and silver-haired bats, and the rabies variants associated with them, account for 70 percent of human cases of rabies and 75 percent of human deaths.[36] What is remarkable is that these bats are rare and represent less than 2 percent of the species of bats reported to the Centers for Disease Control and Prevention each year. In the northwest part of the country, the rabies virus variant associated with the silver-haired bat made up 80 percent of bat-associated human cases.[36] Likewise, in the southeast region of the country, the rabies variant associated with the eastern pipistrelles bat accounted for 89 percent in humans.[36] This high prevalence occurs even though other more common bat species exist in those regions. Why are these rare variants

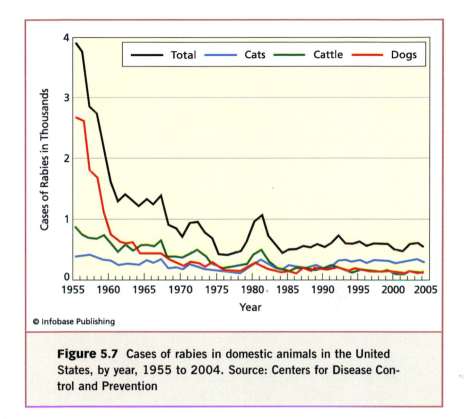

Figure 5.7 Cases of rabies in domestic animals in the United States, by year, 1955 to 2004. Source: Centers for Disease Control and Prevention

found so frequently in humans and other animals? While the answer is not known at this time, experiments have demonstrated that these variants have increased infectivity (they grow better) as compared to variants from canines when grown in cells in the laboratory. This more robust replication may, therefore, facilitate successful infection even after a superficial bite. In many cases, exposure to a rabid animal that does not result in deep penetration (such as a superficial bite), may not lead to rabies. For these two variants, however, apparently such transient exposure is sufficient to initiate a successful rabies infection.

Rodent and lagomorph (i.e., rabbits) cases of rabies make up a very small percentage of cases and represent spillover from reservoir animals. Most reports are for groundhogs in areas where raccoon rabies predominates. Occasionally, rabies is reported in beavers, another large member of the rodent family. Rabies in small rodents is rare, presumably because they seldom survive an attack by a larger rabid carnivore.

DOMESTIC ANIMALS

Rabies reported in domestic animals in 2003 made up 8.6 percent of all animals reported, an increase of 3.7 percent over 2002 (Figure 5.7). Of particular interest to cat and dog owners, rabies in these animals also increased in 2003 as compared to 2002. The largest increase occurred in Texas, followed by Virginia, Oklahoma, Pennsylvania, South Dakota, and New York.[36]

Most of the reported cat cases came from those eastern states where raccoon rabies is enzootic, with the remaining cases in the Central Plains states (Figure 5.8). These latter reports most likely were due to spillover from rabid foxes or rabid skunks in this region of the country. Cat rabies may also be directly related to owners' attitude toward confinement, or lack thereof, of their pets. With the majority of pet cats roaming free, along with their instinctive hunting behavior, they are at increased risk for coming into contact with rabid wildlife.

Reported cases of rabid dogs were only about one-third of that reported for cats in 2003, which probably reflects stricter leash/confinement regulations in each state. Texas, Oklahoma, South Dakota, Puerto Rico, and North Dakota reported the largest number of rabid dogs in 2003 (Figure 5.9). A total of 26 states did not report any incidences of dog rabies. Historically, obtaining rabies from a dog bite was feared the most since these animals were our beloved companions. At least in the United States, dog variants have all but ceased to exist due to strict enforcement of vaccination programs, leash laws, and picking up stray animals that have more chance of coming into contact with rabid animals.

Figure 5.8 Reported cases of rabies in cats, by county and municipio (Puerto Rico), 2004. Source: Centers for Disease Control and Prevention

The total number of rabid cattle reported in 2003, which was 98, was less than the 116 reported in 2002. Interestingly, the distribution of rabies in cattle mirrored that of the range of rabid skunks in the central and Midwestern states and the enzootic raccoon rabies in the east (Figure 5.10). This is a reflection of their being confined to pastures where they are at increased risk of coming into contact with rabid wildlife.

RABIES SEASONAL TRENDS

There are marked seasonal variations of the reported incidences of rabies in various wild animals (Figure 5.11) as well as domestic animals (Figure 5.12). It is interesting to note that

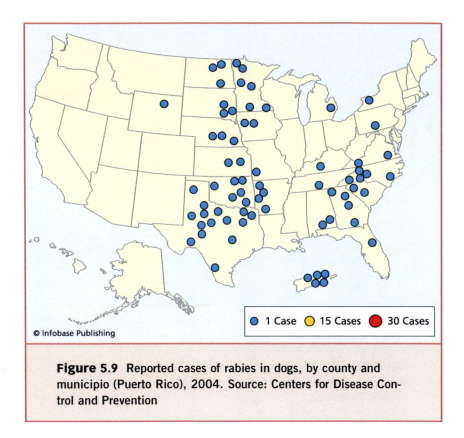

Figure 5.9 Reported cases of rabies in dogs, by county and municipio (Puerto Rico), 2004. Source: Centers for Disease Control and Prevention

rabies in cats is lower in the colder months when owners do not let them roam as often as they do in the warmer months (compare the first three months to the rest of the year in Figure 5.12).

RABIES IN HUMANS IN THE UNITED STATES

Relatively few humans contract rabies in this country. There were five cases in the year 2000, one in 2001, three each in 2002 and 2003, and seven in the first half of 2004. The majority of exposures in humans were due to the bat variants, and there were several deaths attributable to dog variants in countries where there are fewer restrictions concerning dog confinement

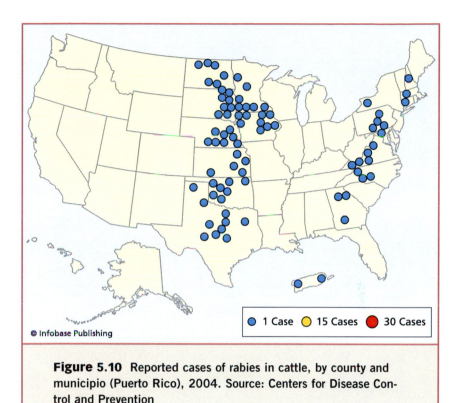

Figure 5.10 Reported cases of rabies in cattle, by county and municipio (Puerto Rico), 2004. Source: Centers for Disease Control and Prevention

or vaccinations compared to the United States. Apparently, none of these victims sought medical help following exposure to dogs in those countries.

The first fatal case in 2003 involved a 25-year-old man in Virginia who died of rabies encephalitis that was due to the type of rabies virus associated with raccoons in the eastern United States.[35] This is significant because it is the first record of an infection of a human by a raccoon variant. Diagnosis in this case was made after the patient died, and family and friends could not confirm any history of an animal bite.

A second fatal human case in 2003 occurred in Puerto Rico and involved a 64-year-old man. It was subsequently shown

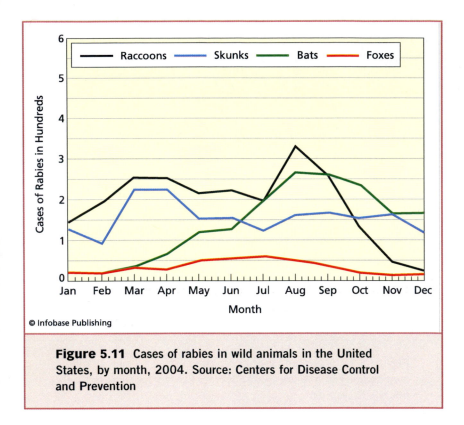

© Infobase Publishing

Figure 5.11 Cases of rabies in wild animals in the United States, by month, 2004. Source: Centers for Disease Control and Prevention

that the rabies variant was that associated with mongooses or unvaccinated dogs.[35] There was history of a dog bite but the victim did not seek medical attention until after the onset of symptoms. This was the first case reported in a human since 1975.

The third fatal case involved a 66-year-old man in California who died of rabies. The variant was identified as the bat variant associated with silver-haired and eastern pipistrelle bats. He had been bitten six weeks previously, but did not seek medical attention.

The above three cases illustrate very clearly the danger of exposure to any animal bite in any country, even in the United States. They also show that a delay in seeking medical help or

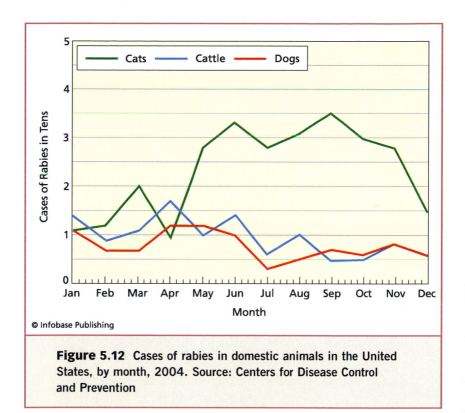

Figure 5.12 Cases of rabies in domestic animals in the United States, by month, 2004. Source: Centers for Disease Control and Prevention

post-exposure treatment can be fatal—an outcome that is totally preventable in this country.

THE UNITED STATES' NORTHERN AND SOUTHERN NEIGHBORS

There were a total of 265 rabies cases in domestic and wild animals in Canada in 2003, which is a 24.4 percent decrease from 349 reports in 2002.[35] This decline was due to fewer cases of rabies in foxes (56.9 percent drop), raccoons (38.5 percent decrease), and skunks (24.8 percent decrease). Other animals reported to be rabid in Canada in 2003 included bats, cattle, cats, dogs, sheep, and horses. One person died from rabies encephalitis that was subsequently found to be a variant of the

Myotis bat. There was no history of a bite. Over 450 people were given post-exposure rabies treatment due to known or possible contact with this patient.

Mexico reported 330 rabies cases in 2003 in domestic and wild animals. This number was almost identical to the 331 cases reported in 2002. Dogs made up the majority of the reports (75 of the 330), although this total was less than the 105 cases reported the previous year. Other animals found to be rabid in Mexico in 2003 included cattle (201 cases), bats, cats, horses, skunks, goats, sheep, foxes, and a badger. There was one human case of rabies in 2003 that was attributable to the dog variant of rabies.

RABIES IN LATIN AMERICA

Most human cases in this part of the world are caused by domestic animals. Molecular studies also suggest the existence of wild animal reservoirs, particularly the mongoose.[37]

Latin America has two main sources of rabies. One is terrestrial animals, primarily the dog—canine rabies is enzootic in most Latin American countries and in the Caribbean. The second is bats, particularly the **haematophagous** bats, those that feed on blood, with the main one being the famous vampire bat. These bats are important because they are found in rural environments close to livestock breeding grounds and spread rabies to livestock. Rabies is also found in **insectivorous** (insect diet) and **frugivorous** (fruit diet) bats. Like the United States, Latin America has several bat rabies variants.

Extensive control measures have been implemented including a dog vaccination program initiated in 1980 with the help of the Pan American Health Organization, whose goal is to eliminate urban dog rabies from this part of the world. With these well-organized, mass-vaccination programs (10 million dogs were vaccinated in one week in Mexico in 1999), the incidence of both animal and human rabies has been drastically reduced.[37]

There are three vampire bat species involved in transmission of rabies. An attempt at disease prevention has included vaccination of cattle and use of anti-coagulants such as diphenadione and warfarin. These are either fed to the cattle as slow-release boluses or mixed with grease and spread on the backs and necks of cattle. The cattle are insensitive to the effects of anti-coagulants while vampire bats are extremely sensitive—they suffer fatal hemorrhages in their wing capillaries when they feed or preen themselves or each other to remove the grease.

RABIES IN ASIA

Dogs are the main rabies reservoir in Asia, with 94 to 98 percent of all human deaths from the disease attributable to dog bites.[37] In fact, the number of human cases here is the highest in the world, particularly in those countries with high population densities (Bangladesh, India, and Pakistan).[37] Recent efforts by some countries, such as Vietnam and Thailand, to implement control programs has decreased the mortality rate. In other countries, however, such as the People's Republic of China and the Philippines, rabies cases have increased in recent years. This increase may be due to several possible reasons including an increase in dog populations, lack of rabies PET, and lack of cost-effective vaccines.[37]

In the year 2000, Thailand reported that 53 percent of human rabies cases were due to dogs that had owners, while 47 percent were caused by stray animals. Although some countries have an organized program for slaughtering stray dogs, these programs are not widespread and there is resistance to this practice in some areas for cultural and religious reasons. Stray dog programs are different for each country and adapted for their particular needs. In India, for example, 97,000 stray dogs were captured between 1993 and 1998 (out of a total dog population of about 25 million). They were neutered, vaccinated against rabies, and released. In theory, if neutering programs are conducted regularly, they could lead to stabilization of the stray dog population within five to seven years.[37]

Even in countries where there are rabies control programs in place, only a few have systems of surveillance/control that are considered satisfactory in terms of identifying and reducing animal and human rabies, including Indonesia, Malaysia, the People's Republic of China, the Philippines, Sri Lanka, Thailand, and Vietnam.[37] Unfortunately, many such programs are initiated piecemeal and only in those regions where trained personnel and diagnostic facilities exist.

Dogs serve as the primary reservoir animal in Asia. Wolves, jackals, mongoose, or bats have all been suggested as additional wild animal reservoirs, but there are no data to support this

MOTHER NATURE'S INFLUENCE

Sri Lanka is an island nation where rabies is endemic in most districts. Rabies exists in dogs and represents a stable, geographically isolated virus population. This latter point is significant because such virus populations are susceptible to extinction. Since there are no wild animal reservoirs of rabies on this island nation, rabies could be eliminated.

Due to high numbers of human deaths (about 400 each year during the 1970s), a rabies prevention and control program was instituted. This included regular dog vaccinations and the availability of modern rabies vaccines for humans following exposure to rabies or a suspect animal. This program has significantly reduced the number of human deaths to approximately 75 annually for the years 2001-2003. It is quite probable, therefore, with continuous, rigid implementation of this program, the grand goal of rabies elimination from the entire island could be realized.

Natural events interfered, however, and the devastating tsunami of December 2004 has put a stranglehold on rabies hypothesis, although there are limited data from the Philippines suggesting the presence of a rabies virus in bats. Additional research using epidemiological and molecular analyses on a large scale would be needed to confirm this hypothesis.

RABIES IN AFRICA

Dogs are the main reservoir of rabies in Africa. They represent greater than 75 percent of all rabid animals in most African countries. Many human victims are children under 10 years old. The involvement of wild animals in the transmission cycle of rabies in Africa has not been well studied. This is due to other public health priorities, including acquired immune deficiency syndrome (AIDS), malaria, and tuberculosis.[37]

control efforts in the southern part of Sri Lanka. In the aftermath of the tsunami, over 100,000 dogs are thought to have lost contact with their owners or the communities where they belonged in the southern and eastern districts. As a result, these dogs are now roaming free while still others are in refugee camps. To make matters worse, the rabies diagnostic laboratory that served the southern province was washed away and destroyed. It is likely that the progress made in reducing human fatalities due to rabies will disappear, that the ambitious goal of removing this disease forever from the island will be delayed, and the number of rabies cases will increase since so many animals are unsupervised and likely to come into contact with humans, particularly children, in the camps. Lack of functional diagnostic facilities also compounds the risks. Authorities have proposed a mass vaccination campaign of dogs in this region of Sri Lanka, but, as of this date, the vaccines are still not yet available.

A national rabies control program is in place in Tunisia that was initiated in 1982. A campaign of dog vaccination was conducted every two years, and then changed to annual vaccination due to rapid dog population turnover. A major part of the success of this program was the fact that quality vaccines were produced locally. The best measure of how successful this program has been is that only 178 cases of rabies occurred in animals and one in humans in 1999.

In 2002, data from Morocco showed 446 cases of animal rabies and 23 human deaths. These latter cases occurred predominantly in rural and suburban regions and were due to a dog variant of rabies. Of the people who died as a result of rabies between 1995 and 2001 in Morocco, 86 percent had not received post-exposure rabies treatment or vaccine.

Data collected in Tanzania demonstrate that the number of human rabies cases is underestimated. This study indicated there were 4.9 human deaths per 100,000 people, which is 100 times more that the number officially recorded for this country.[38, 39] This drastically different number was based on data gathered from:

1. the incidence of wounds from animal bites

2. the accuracy of the rabies diagnosis

3. the number of bite wounds received/person

4. frequency of post-exposure treatment[39]

The study also showed that the high incidence of human rabies was due to:

1. the high cost of post-exposure treatment

2. the rapid growth of human and dog populations

3. the increasing mobility of rural populations

4. the decline in the infrastructure and resources needed for disease control[37]

Humans are at significant risk for rabies in South Africa, Angola, Botswana, Namibia, Zambia, and Zimbabwe. In addition, the situation is complicated by rabies transmission cycles in wild animals independent of canines and by the presence of rabies-related viruses in wild cats. Dog-associated rabies has also been found in jackals and bat-eared foxes. Similarly, it is significant that numerous rabies-related virus isolates in shrews and bats infected with the Lagos and Makola viruses were discovered in Nigeria.

The incidence of dog rabies is increasing in sub-Saharan Africa, because few successful vaccination programs have been initiated in the last 20 years. There have been some attempts at oral vaccination in jackals, African wild dogs, and domestic dogs.

RABIES IN EUROPE

Since the 1930s in Europe, the main reservoir for rabies is the red fox followed by the raccoon dog in Central and Baltic Europe. When rabies is introduced into a rabies-free area, the fox population rapidly declines. Due to their high reproductive potential, however, the fox population recovers quickly. With the exception of certain islands (Britain, Ireland) and large peninsulas (Norway and Sweden), most of Europe has become infected with rabies.[37]

Early control efforts, such as reducing the numbers of foxes, did not prevent spread of the rabies virus. Oral vaccines, however, scattered throughout fox habitats, have been successful at breaking the transmission cycle. Use of this vaccine began in Switzerland in 1978. To date, seven countries are considered rabies-free as a result of these programs:

1. Finland and the Netherlands, since 1991

2. Italy, since 1997

3. Switzerland, since 1998

4. France, since 2000

5. Belgium and Luxembourg, since 2001[37]

Human cases of rabies in Europe are generally due to the following causes:

1. canine rabies contracted in a non-European country

2. infection by a rabid indigenous or imported wild or domestic animal (mainly Russia and the Ukraine)

3. infection by a rabid bat (four human cases since 1977)[37]

Since 1954, several rabies-related viruses associated with bats have been discovered. It is now known that bat rabies covers most of Europe, from Russia to Spain, particularly in the coastal regions. Spillover into terrestrial animals is rare, with only two cases found in sheep in Denmark and one case of a stone marten in Germany.

RABIES-FREE COUNTRIES

It should be obvious by now, that the majority of countries have rabies in one form or another (i.e., terrestrial animals or bats). There are, however, several countries, mostly islands, that are considered rabies-free. The list includes Japan, New Zealand, Britain, Ireland, Fiji, Barbados, Maldives, Iceland, and Scandinavia. Strict enforcement of quarantine laws of dogs and cats for various periods of time (depending on the country) before entry has been used effectively to exclude rabies from Japan, Hawaii, and other areas.

Interestingly, rabies had never become endemic in wild animals in England and was eradicated from dogs in 1902.

Rabies was reestablished in the dog population in the United Kingdom in 1918 and again eradicated in 1922. Since that time, there has been no rabies in this country. There was, however, a single bat found to be infected with a European bat virus variant, but this one discovery has not changed the rabies-free status of England.

Australia was rabies-free until the discovery of a rabies-related virus, designated as Australian bat lyssavirus, in 1996.[40] This bat virus was isolated from a frugivorous bat (i.e. fruit bat or flying fox) of the Megachiroptera family. Since this initial discovery, other frugivorous as well as insectivorous bats have been shown to be reservoirs for this virus. The range of this virus extends along the entire east coast of Australia. To date, there have been two human deaths attributed to the Australian bat lyssavirus. Imported dogs and cats are being quarantined to prevent this virus from becoming endemic in wild and domestic animals.

6

Diagnosis of Rabies

A hallmark discovery in the field of rabies diagnosis came in 1903 by Italian physician, Adelchi Negri, who was also a pathologist and a microbiologist. His initial studies were in **cytology** (study of cell structure), **histology** (microscopic study of animal or plant tissues), **hematology** (study of blood), **protozoology** (study of single-celled organisms known as proto-zoans), and **hygiene** (science of establishing and maintaining health). Then in 1903, he began research on the etiology of rabies—the cause of rabies still had not yet been clearly demonstrated at that time. What he discovered, and later described to other scientists, were **inclusion bodies** within the brains of rabies-infected animals. Negri described them as round or oval intracellular structures located in the **cytoplasm** (the area outside of the nucleus) of infected nerve cells. These **intracytoplasmic** inclusions vary in size from 0.25 to 27 microns and are found most often, although not exclusively, in the hippocampus, cerebellum, thalamus, and spinal cord areas of the CNS. These inclusion bodies were found to be a persistent feature in the nerve cells of infected humans and animals and made possible a correct diagnosis. In honor of this scientific contribution, rabies inclusion bodies now bear his name and are known as **Negri bodies** (Figure 6.1).

SUITABLE TYPES OF SAMPLES FOR RABIES TESTING

The brain has been, and remains, the primary tissue of choice for rabies testing. Of course, the brain can only be obtained for laboratory exami-nation from dead animals or humans. Particular regions, as mentioned above, are preferred and can be harvested once the skull has been opened and the brain removed.

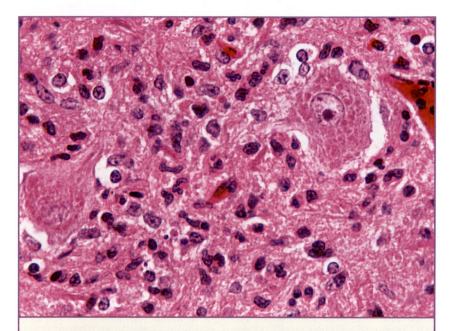

Figure 6.1 Negri bodies characteristic of rabies (seen here as dark spots) are present within this sample of brain tissue from a patient who died of rabies. Source: Centers for Disease Control and Prevention

What then can we do if a patient suspected of rabies exposure is alive? What samples can be used for a diagnostic test in that situation? For humans, there is a sense of urgency since it is necessary to initiate treatment quickly as well as to reduce the number of contacts with this person. This latter point is important because a positive rabies diagnosis would result in all people who have had contact with the patient being treated as well. Alternative samples, therefore, have to be collected since the brain cannot be used.

One alternative specimen from living patients would be the skin from specific regions of the body. Skin samples are obtained in the form of skin biopsies from areas of the neck, particularly where there are abundant hair follicles. Areas rich in hair follicles are good places to sample because the virus can be detected in the nerves around hair follicles. Testing skin samples for rabies has been reported to yield accurate results 60 to 100 percent of the time.[41] This type of sample may be most useful for detection in the early stages of a possible infection, as a part of the laboratory examination of a biting animal, or when it is impractical or impossible to obtain the brain of, for example, a large animal in the field.[42]

Once it was discovered that rabies virus was present on the cornea during the final stages of the disease, the cornea was used as another alternative specimen for rabies testing in living patients. Cornea testing was first performed on mice

IMPRESSION SMEARS

Corneal cell smears for rabies diagnostic testing are not the only type of smears scientists use in the laboratory. Impression smears can also be made from other tissues and is done routinely in many veterinary diagnostic laboratories around the country. These smears are then used for fluorescent antibody (FAT) testing for a variety of different viruses (more on this later!).

How are impression smears from tissues made? Let's say you are a veterinary technician in a state-run veterinary diagnostic laboratory and, during the necropsy, or post-mortem exam, of a dead animal, such as a cow, the pathologist hands you a petri dish with pieces of kidney, lung, intestine, and spleen in it. What do you do? First, think safety. To process the tissue safely, you will need to put on rubber gloves, a lab coat, and transfer the petri dish to a special type of work desk with a hood called a type II biological safety cabinet. This cabinet filters the air as it circulates so that the environment and subsequently in humans.[43] It is, however, considered less reliable under field conditions.[43] Samples are obtained by making corneal impression smears, which is done by lightly touching a glass microscope slide to the center of the cornea, thereby transferring cells onto the slide. These cells can then be used for testing.

As you already know, during the later stages of a rabies infection, the virus spreads from the CNS to other organs and tissues of the body via the nerves innervating these areas. Of particular importance, the virus spreads to the salivary glands and replicates in cells of the salivary glands. As a result, large amounts of rabies virus are present in the saliva before clinical signs appear. Therefore, saliva and salivary glands are additional sources of samples that can be used for testing. A

inside the hood is sterile. Then using sterile forceps and a scalpel blade, you cut the tissues in a way that gives you a nice, straight cut through the organ. Picking the tissue up with the forceps, blot it several times in the petri dish to remove excess moisture and immediately blot it onto a glass slide. No need to press really hard or to twist the tissue on the slide; just an even pressure for a second or two is sufficient to transfer cells from the cut side of the tissue onto the slide. Once this is done for all tissues, the slides are air-dried, the tissues "fixed" or made to permanently adhere to the slide with an acetone bath for ten minutes, and air-dried again. Now they are ready for analysis by FAT. Our example above was a cow, so the pathologist may ask you to test the tissues for bovine viral diarrhea virus, an economically important virus that causes several problems in beef and dairy cattle such as diarrhea, abortion, stomatitis, immunosuppression, pneumonia, and gastrointestinal erosion.

problem, however, is that the virus is not consistently detected in the saliva of patients.

Specimens that could assist in the diagnosis of rabies are not limited to those mentioned above. Other specimens that have been used include cerebrospinal fluid, tonsils, and various non-neural organs of animals and humans. Examples of rabies-positive non-neural tissue include muscle fibers of the heart, tongue, and larynx in samples from Mexico and the Peoples Republic of China.[44]

INITIAL TESTING FOR RABIES

Histology involves the use of a number of different stains that are placed on sections of tissues. Stains highlight the cells within the tissue and allow the scientist to see them through a microscope. To take the analysis of stained tissues a step further, a trained microscopist, such as a pathologist, would be able to identify changes in tissues due to disease—this would include the staining of cells not normally found in a healthy tissue. This type of analysis is called **histopathology**.

Two of the most common stains used today by pathologists are eosin and hematoxylin. Figure 6.1 shows a very thin section of brain tissue stained with these two stains. Note also in this figure, eosin and hematoxylin highlight more than just Negri bodies. The numerous dark shapes above the infected neuron are immune system cells that have infiltrated the brain due to infection and are part of the body's inflammatory response to defend against foreign organisms. A pathologist, therefore, would be able to identify inflammatory cells as abnormal for that tissue and would know there is a current infection.

In his research on rabies, Adelchi Negri used stains that highlighted tissues and observed inclusion bodies within rabies-infected cells. Histological analysis of tissues to identify Negri bodies was used for many years, even into the 1950s, and was considered the defining diagnostic test for positive

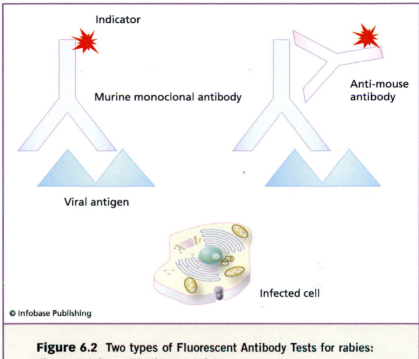

Indicator

Murine monoclonal antibody

Anti-mouse
antibody

Viral antigen

Infected cell

© Infobase Publishing

Figure 6.2 Two types of Fluorescent Antibody Tests for rabies:
direct, at left, and indirect, at right.

identification of a rabies infection. It is now known, however,
that only about 50 to 80 percent of rabies-positive animals actually have Negri bodies.[3] This means that at least 20 percent of all
samples tested would yield false-negative results, a rate that is
totally unacceptable as a diagnostic test. What was needed was a
diagnostic test that was more sensitive (i.e., a negative test really
means no disease) and more specific (i.e., a positive test means
there really is disease) with no false negatives.

FAT (FLUORESCENT ANTIBODY TEST)

FAT is an abbreviation for a technique that has become the
modern-day standard diagnostic test for rabies and is used in

laboratories all over the world. FAT stands for Fluorescent Antibody Test and is able to detect nearly 100 percent of rabies-positive samples. This test, therefore, meets the criteria mentioned in the preceding paragraph for a more reliable test and has replaced testing for the presence of Negri bodies. FAT relies on the use of antibodies to identify specific

HOW DOES A FLOURESCENCE MICROSCOPE WORK?

Let's begin by defining what the word fluorescence means. This is the process in which some molecules, such as the indicators attached to antibodies, become excited by absorbing light at one wavelength and subsequently giving off light of a longer wavelength. It is this emitted light of a longer wavelength that is viewed in the fluorescence microscope. In addition, this entire reaction ceases as soon as the light source is turned off. The molecules or indicators that absorb light are called chromophores. There are many different chromophores in existence today and they are widely used in laboratories for research, clinical, or diagnostic purposes.

Now let's look at the microscope. One essential requirement is that it comes equipped with a combination of mirrors and filter cubes. The filters are capable of exciting fluorescent molecules when light passes through them as it travels to the sample, and the mirrors direct the emitted light to the eyepiece of the microscope.

These microscopes also require a light source, one that is powerful enough to generate excitation of chromophores. Popular today are mercury or xenon arc lamps, both of which produce high-intensity light capable of causing fluorescence.

Let's put this all together. Light from the mercury lamp passes through the filter cube and hits the tissue. The indicator molecules attached to antibodies give off light of a parts of viral proteins (called **antigens**) and are specific only for that one antigen (Figure 6.2). Two types of FAT assays are depicted in this figure, direct and indirect. The direct FAT, which is very fast, is used for rabies diagnostic examinations, while the indirect FAT, which takes more time, is also very sensitive, but is mostly used on cells grown in a laboratory.

longer wavelength. Mirrors then direct the emitted light (apple-green as seen in Figure 6.3) to the eyepiece of the microscope where a trained pathologist is viewing the tissue.

Other considerations include image brightness. It is easy to say the tissue in Figure 6.3 is positive for rabies because the amount of virus antigen is large and fluoresces a very bright apple-green (i.e., the sample is a strong positive). But what if it were only weakly fluorescing? How would you distinguish a weak positive from "background" fluorescence or "noise" (antibodies with attached chromophores sometimes don't wash away during the FAT procedure and create background fluorescence)? This is a problem indeed and, in fact, is one of the shortcomings of this technique. So, for weakly fluorescing tissues, image brightness is very important and can help in distinguishing real positives from background noise.

Another handy feature of fluorescence microscopes is the ability to take pictures of what you are viewing through the eyepiece. Today, digital cameras are attached to microscopes and are also linked directly to a computer. Not only is it possible to visualize what you are seeing on the large monitor screen, but it is also possible to capture to the computer's hard drive any image you want.

In figure 6.2, consider the infected cell to be brain tissue (or any infected tissue). If the brain is infected with rabies virus, viral antigens will be present on the surface of the brain cells. Onto this tissue are added antibodies specific for rabies virus antigens. In addition, attached to the top of each antibody is a special indicator molecule that absorbs light. The antibodies recognize the virus antigens and bind to them. After extensive washing, only those antibodies attached to antigens will remain—if no viral antigen is present, then all of the antibodies will be washed away. The tissue is then examined under a special type of microscope, called a fluorescence microscope, to determine if rabies antigen is present in the tissue. The light on the microscope hits the indicator, which then appears apple-green in color (Figure 6.3). Hence, apple-green fluorescence indicates a positive result for a rabies infection. Because of its high sensitivity, specificity, and speed, the direct FAT has become the "gold standard" for rabies testing. This simply means that all other rabies tests measure their level of success against the FAT test.

IMMUNOCHEMISTRY

The term "immunohistochemistry" can be broken down into parts to determine its meaning. The first part "immuno," refers to immune system molecules (antibodies); the second, "histo," means that tissue sections are involved; and the third, "chemistry," indicates the use of a chemical reaction. Immunohistochemistry, or IHC, therefore, is the use of antibodies to detect rabies virus in tissue sections. Next, an **enzyme (a protein that speeds up chemical reactions)**, which is attached to the antibody, acts on its target or **substrate** to yield a color change (the color change is the chemical reaction). IHC is very similar to the direct FAT method except that, instead of an indicator molecule attached to the antibody, IHC uses an antibody with an attached enzyme.

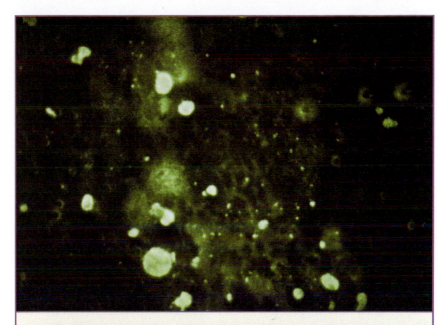

Figure 6.3 This immunofluorescent micrograph reveals a positive result for the presence of rabies virus antigens in this specimen. Source: Centers for Disease Control and Prevention

For IHC, very thin sections of tissue are fixed (i.e. preserved) in a preservative called **formalin**. Next, antibodies, with attached enzyme, are added, washed, and followed by the addition of substrate. The enzyme acts on the substrate to form a colored precipitate, which is easily visible under a microscope. If the tissue is not infected with rabies virus, the antibodies are washed away and there is no color change.

There are several major drawbacks to IHC that prevent it from becoming more widely used. One is the length of time it takes to perform this procedure compared to the direct FAT. A second is that the reagents needed to do IHC are very expensive. Lastly, IHC reagents are considered toxic or carcinogenic (i.e., cancer causing).

LATEX AGGLUTINATION

As good as the direct FAT is, some tissue may not be suitable for examination by this method. One example of an unsuitable sample is rotten tissue. An alternative test that could be used on degraded specimens and that has shown promise on dog saliva and brain tissue is the latex agglutination test.[45] This method utilizes latex beads coated with antibodies specific for rabies virus. Beads and saliva are mixed together and a white precipitate forms if the virus is present in the saliva. This precipitate is readily visible by the naked eye. If no virus is present, then the bead and saliva mixture remains clear. Saliva is easy to use for this test since it is already in solution. But how would this test be performed on tissue? The tissue can be turned into a homogeneous liquid that is suitable for use in the latex agglutination test basically by placing it in a blender and mixing it. Kitchen blenders would not be used to work with a suspected rabies case because of the high risk of spreading contaminated tissue through the air, but there are a variety of methods to homogenize tissues that are much safer, such as a mortar and pestle or a stomacher, a specialized laboratory blender.

Compared to the direct FAT method, latex agglutination exhibited very high sensitivity and specificity rates. Additional studies with this method are being done to improve these factors even more.

LABORATORY ANIMALS

In some countries, where rabies is endemic, the decision to treat humans for rabies exposure relies heavily on detecting the virus in the dog or other animal responsible for the bite. This would not be an issue in the United States, but general use of such expensive treatments in poorer countries would be an economical burden.

Because of this, initial tests (e.g., direct FAT) serve only as a first step, and any samples yielding negative or ambiguous (i.e., can't call it positive or negative) results will require additional testing in suckling mice (less than three days old). The specimen, usually brain tissue or salivary glands, is homogenized and then used for intracerebral inoculation (i.e. injected directly into the brain) into the mice. If virus is present, it will replicate. The mouse brain, now containing large amounts of virus, can be easily tested for rabies by standard techniques. Use of mice is time-consuming (up to 15 days) but is considered definitive as it demonstrates the presence of virus. Use of suckling mice is preferred over weanling or adult mice because they are more susceptible to rabies virus.

CELL CULTURE SYSTEMS

Because of more and more restrictions on the use of animals in laboratories, some countries, such as the United States and Europe, have been phasing out the use of mice for rabies testing and using cell culture systems instead.

A cell culture system simply refers to growing cells, such as kidney cells or mouse neuron cells (called neuroblastoma cells), in a sterile plastic container (Figure 6.4). A homogenized sample is added to the cells and within four days, the presence or absence of rabies can be determined by examining the cells using FAT. In developing countries, however, the use of mice will continue because cell culture requires expensive equipment and reagents, specialized facilities, and highly trained personnel.

RT-PCR

A molecular technique, with sensitivity and specificity equal to FAT, that detects rabies virus genetic material is called Reverse Transcription-Polymerase Chain Reaction (RT-PCR). While these may look like complicated words, they really are not. Let's look first at the second half of this series of words. "Polymerase" refers to the use of an enzyme (polymerase) that is involved in making more DNA (i.e. replicating or synthesizing

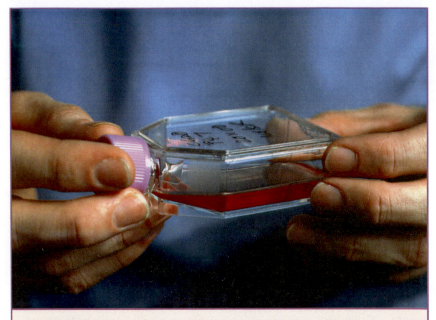

Figure 6.4 A culture flask used for growing cells. © James King-Holmes/Photo Researchers, Inc.

more DNA). "Chain Reaction" refers to the same DNA synthesis step being repeated over and over, millions of times. As you already know, the genetic material of rabies virus is RNA. In order to use RNA in a polymerase chain reaction, it must first be converted into DNA, called copy DNA or cDNA, and this is done with another enzyme called Reverse Transcriptase. Hence, we have a Reverse Transcriptase enzyme that turns a part of the rabies virus RNA into cDNA, which is then used in the Polymerase Chain Reaction. Because it is repeated numerous times, it results in amplification of a specific portion of the cDNA (Figure 6.5).

Once the RT-PCR assay is completed, it is possible to visualize the amplified DNA. This is done by first placing the RT-PCR mixture onto a special type of medium called agarose

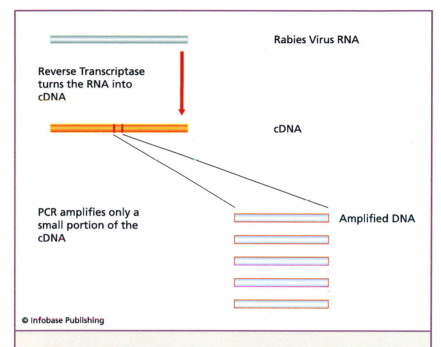

Rabies Virus RNA

Reverse Transcriptase
turns the RNA into
cDNA

cDNA

PCR amplifies only a
small portion of the
cDNA

Amplified DNA

© Infobase Publishing

Figure 6.5 The enzyme reverse transcriptase converts the rabies
virus genomic RNA (green rectangle) into cDNA (gold rectangle),
which can then be used in the polymerase chain reaction (PCR).
PCR is normally used to amplify only a small portion of the DNA
as indicated by the red vertical lines. Blue rectangles represent
products of repeated rounds of DNA synthesis during PCR and
results in amplification of the small portion of DNA. Source:
Thomas Kienzle.

(similar in consistency to gelatin). Second, an electric current
is applied to the agarose, which causes the DNA to move in the
agarose—the distance it moves is based on its size. Third, the
agarose is then soaked in a chemical called ethidium bromide,
which binds DNA. Finally, because ethidium bromide fluoresces when exposed to ultra-violet light, the agarose is placed
on an ultra-violet light box and a picture is taken of the fluorescing DNA.

The major advantage of RT-PCR is that it can be used on any sample—liquid, tissue, and even rotten specimens—and because of this, it will eventually replace the direct FAT as the method of choice for rabies infection diagnosis.

7

Prevention/ Vaccination/Treatment

Rabies is a disease for which there are sufficient remedies to prevent development of clinical illness. In most industrialized countries, control of human rabies has occurred, mainly due to available treatment upon exposure to a rabid animal, mandatory vaccination of pets, institution of oral vaccination programs of wildlife, and preemptive vaccination for humans at high risk.

Is this the case for the rest of the world? Unfortunately, the answer is no. Thousands die in developing countries each year, despite the World Health Organization designating rabies as a priority for control in these countries.[46] One reason for this is the low level of political commitment of governments to consider rabies important enough to warrant spending scarce resources. This is partly due to the fact that rabies exposure is underreported, which leads to rabies being considered rare or insignificant.[47] Another factor is the expense involved in the treatment of rabies. In addition, many consider rabies control to be the responsibility of the veterinarian community.[47] Studies designed to look at the impact of rabies on public health in terms of cost and estimated years of life lost prematurely have demonstrated the cost-effectiveness and cost-benefits of rabies control programs, even exceeding the impact of other high-profile diseases.[47, 48]

TREATMENT AND PREVENTION IN HUMANS
Avoiding rabies is obviously the best way to ensure you will never get the disease, because, in almost all cases there is no treatment or cure once symptoms appear. One way to do this is to get a vaccine. A vaccine is

Figure 7.1 Portrait of Louis Pasteur. © Explorer/Photo Researchers, Inc.

defined as a preparation of a weakened or killed pathogen (e.g., virus or bacterium) or a part of the disease-causing organism that, when administered to a person, initiates an immune response and the body makes antibodies to the vaccine. These antibodies will protect against disease if the vaccinated person comes into contact with a wild type or field version of the pathogen. Vaccines can be given as a pre-exposure measure to people who are in high-risk jobs, such as veterinarians, farmers, research or diagnostic laboratory personnel, or international travelers. In addition, one can obtain post-exposure vaccination after a bite from an animal, and if given soon enough, disease can be avoided.

The original rabies vaccine, developed by Louis Pasteur, was desiccated spinal cords from infected rabbits (Figure 7.1). For many years, such nerve- or brain-derived vaccines were commonly used to protect against rabies. Fortunately for people in this country, newer, more efficient, and safer vaccines have been developed that replace the older vaccines. Due to costs or lack of appropriate technology, however, developing countries continue to use the older form of vaccination.

One type of modern-day vaccine used in this country is the human diploid cell vaccine (HDCV). This vaccine is made by growing the virus in human cells, concentrating it, and then inactivating it with a chemical. A second type is known as rabies vaccine adsorbed (RVA) and is generated by growing the rabies virus in rhesus monkey cells followed by inactivation and adsorption to a chemical called aluminum phosphate. The last vaccine approved for human use is called purified chick embryo cell vaccine (PCEC), which is prepared by growing the virus in **embryonated eggs** (fertilized eggs with a developing embryo) followed by concentrating and inactivating it. All of these vaccines can be given by intramuscular injection, while only the HDCV can be administered intradermally, or into the skin, as well.

Table 7. 1 gives a schedule for persons receiving pre-exposure vaccination and boosters. Note that this type of vaccination does not preclude the need to seek medical treatment upon exposure to rabies or a rabid animal. For persons at continued risk, boosters are recommended as well as periodic checks of antibody levels in their blood.

Table 7.1 Rabies Pre-exposure Prophylaxis Schedule—United States, 1999

Types of Vaccination	Route	Regimine
Primary	Intramuscular	HDCV, PCEC, or RVA; 1.0 mL (deltoid area), one each on days 0,* 7, and 21 or 28
	Intradermal	HDCV; 0.1 mL, one each on days 0,* 7, and 21 or 28
Booster	Intramuscular	HDCV, PCEC, or RVA; 1.0 mL (deltoid area), day 0* only
	Intradermal	HDCV, 0.1 mL, day 0* only

HDCV=human diploid cell vaccine; PCEC=purified chick embryo cell vaccine; RVA=rabies vaccine adsorbed.
* Day 0 is the day the first dose of vaccine is administered.

Post-exposure treatment is more complicated than simply receiving a shot of vaccine, although that is a part of the overall therapy regimen. The treatment schedule for those previously vaccinated as well as not previously vaccinated is presented in Table 7.2. Cleaning the bite wound with soap and water is always the first step as it helps to reduce the risk of a bacterial infection. Irrigating the wound with 70 percent ethanol or povidone solutions may actually reduce the chance of transmission from a bite. After this, the victim should seek medical treatment that will include a dose of **rabies immunoglobulin** (RIG), a solution of blood proteins with high levels of anti-rabies antibodies, so that these antibodies will be present until the victim begins making his or her own antibodies. RIG is followed by administration of an anti-rabies vaccine. Combined, these steps are called post-exposure treatment or PET. Remember, PET is for all persons who may have come into contact with any animal (or human!) whose rabies

Table 7.2 Rabies Post-exposure Prophylaxis Schedule—United States, 1999

Vaccination Status	Treatment	Regimine
Not previously vaccinated	Wound cleansing	All post-exposure treatment should begin with immediate, thorough cleansing of all wounds with soap and water. If available, a virucidal agent such as a povidone-iodine solution should be used to irrigate the wounds.
	RIG	Administer 20 IU/kg body weight. If anatomically feasible, the full dose should be infiltrated around the wounds(s) and any remaining volume should be administered at an anatomical site distant from vaccine administration. Also, RIG should not be administered in the same syringe as vaccine. Because RIG might partially suppress active production of antibody, no more than the recommended dose should be given.
	Vaccine	HDCV, RVA, or PCEC 1.0 mL, IM (deltoid area**), one each on days 0 and 3, 7, 14, and 28.
Previously vaccinated***	Wound cleansing	All post-exposure treatment should begin with immediate, thorough cleansing of all wounds with soap and water. If available, a virucidal agent such as a povidone-iodine solution should be used to irrigate the wounds.
	RIG	RIG should **not** be administered.
	Vaccine	HDCV, RVA, or PCEC 1.0 mL, IM deltoid area+), one each on days 0 and 3.

HDCV=human diploid cell vaccine; PCEC=purified chick embryo cell vaccine; RIG=rabies immune globulin; RVA=rabies vaccine adsorbed; IM, intramuscular. These regimens are applicable for all age groups, including children.

** The deltoid area is the only acceptable site of vaccination for adults and older children. For younger children, the outer aspect of the thigh may be used. Vaccine should never be administered in the gluteal area.

*** Day 0 is the day the first dose of vaccine is administered.

Table 7.3 Rabies Biologics—United States

Human Rabies Vaccine	Product Name	Manufacturer
Human diploid cell vaccine Vaccins,(HFCV) 　Intramuscular 　Intradermal	 Imovax Rabies Imovax Rabies I.D	Pasteur-Meriux Serum et Connaught Laboratories, Inc. (800) VACCINE (822-2463)
Rabies vaccine adsorbed (RVA) 　Intramuscular Purified chick embryo cell 　Intramuscular	 Adsorbed (RVA) RabAvert	BioPort Corporation (517) 335-8120 Chiron Corporation vaccine (PCEC) CHIRON8 (800) 244-7668
Rabies immune globulin(RIG)	Imogam Rabies-HT BayRab	Pasteur-Merieux Serum et Vaccins, Connaught Laboratories, Inc. (800) VACCINE (822-2463) Bayer Corporation Pharmaceutical Div. (800) 288-8370

status is suspect. Even if there is no visible bite wound, you still may need PET—delaying or avoiding medical attention could cost you your life. Table 7.3 lists sources of approved human rabies vaccines and RIG (together known as rabies biologics) for use in the United States.

As with any medical treatment, significant costs can be incurred when treating rabies. Even though human deaths are infrequent in this country, the costs associated with prevention, detection, and control exceed $300 million per year. This money is used to vaccinate pets, ensure public health by picking up strays, maintain rabies-testing laboratories, and provide PET. Records are not available on the actual number of PETs given to people each year, but it is estimated to be more than 40,000. While the cost varies from state to state, a course of rabies immune globulin and five doses of vaccine given over a four-week period may cost over $1,000 per person.

TREATMENT AND PREVENTION IN DOMESTIC ANIMALS

There are several vaccines available for domestic animals, which are very similar to those used in humans, although more options are available for animal use (see Table 7.4 for the various vaccines licensed for animal use in the United States). The preferred animal vaccines are produced in cell culture because they can provide stable, long-lasting immunity—other types, such as nerve-tissue vaccines, are being phased out. Combined vaccines are a slight variation on the vaccination scheme and are available to inoculate dogs and cats against several different pathogens at the same time.

In addition to rabies antigens, combined vaccines for dogs also contain antigens for canine distemper virus, canine adenovirus type 1, *Leptospira*, and canine parvovirus. For cats, a combination of antigens from feline panleukopenia virus, feline calicivirus, and feline parvovirus are available.

Imagine you've been bitten by a neighborhood dog. What do you do? First and foremost, seek the advice of a doctor (after washing the wound with soap and water) for possible PET. You'll probably also want to know the vaccination history of the animal—this information will be helpful to the medical professional handling your case. Even if the animal that bit you appears in good health and has a history of rabies vaccination, there is no guarantee that it is rabies-free. Animal vaccine failures can occur and may be due to substandard quality of vaccine, poor animal health, and the possibility that a single dose of rabies vaccine may not always provide long-lasting protection. It may be necessary, therefore, particularly if the offending animal is wild, to humanely kill it and test its brain for rabies. A pet dog or cat that bites someone and is subsequently captured, can be held for 10 days (see Table 7.5 for guidelines for observation or treatment) for observation as the progression of rabies is certain in these animals—it is less certain in other animals and the 10-day observation may not apply. If an animal remains healthy during this period, the PET can always be discontinued.

Besides vaccinating your pets, what else can you do to protect them from rabies? For dogs and cats, vaccination is mandatory, but what about other types of pets, such as rabbits or pet rodents? This is especially important since all pets are at

WHAT ELSE CAN YOU DO?

Is vaccination the only way to prevent disease or the spread of disease? No, it is not. There is something you do multiple times a day that will get rid of disease-causing organisms. Can you think of what it is? Hopefully, this action is something you do each and every time you use the bathroom. If you haven't figured it out already, it is the simple, but very important, act of washing your hands with soap and water. This is the single easiest way to maintain good health. Rubbing your hands under the faucet with soap for 20 seconds can remove the flu virus, cold virus, diarrhea-causing viruses, and other organisms that might inadvertently be transferred to your mouth or eyes from your fingers. Is this really important? According to the Centers for Disease Control and Prevention, people not washing their hands contributes to almost half of all food-borne disease outbreaks.

The American Society for Microbiology conducted a survey of public restrooms to determine who does and does not wash their hands. Want to see some of their very interesting findings? Researchers lingered in public restrooms in four cities and silently counted the number of people who washed up. They found that men wash less often than women: only 64 percent of men washed their hands in New York's Penn Station, compared to 92 percent of women. The best hygiene was observed in San Francisco's Ferry Terminal Farmer's risk of coming into contact with rabid wild animals if they are not indoor pets. A good way to protect them is to use double-cage housing if they are housed outside.

On the other hand, if a pet rabbit has been in contact with a wild animal, it will be necessary to quarantine the pet for six months of observation. This is particularly relevant if there is

Market and Chicago's Museum of Science and Industry, where 88 percent of adults washed their hands after using the public restroom. During an Atlanta Braves baseball game at Turner Field, greater than 25 percent of adults did not wash up after using the public facilities. And these results were when people were watching! Imagine how the rates might drop with no observer present! A phone survey conducted by Harris Interactive reported that 91 percent of adults said they always wash their hands in public restrooms, 77 percent said they washed before handling or eating food, but only 32 percent washed their hands after coughing or sneezing.

Can you think of something that might be in your pocket right now that everybody wants more of, and nobody ever has enough of, yet is touched by hundreds or thousands of different people? Yes, it's money. Imagine how many people might have touched the dollar bill that's in your wallet, but had not washed their hands.

It appears there is plenty of room for improvement in this country in terms of personal hygiene. So, don't be so busy that you forget to wash your hands—wash them and wash them often.

Source: American Society for Microbiology, "Women better at hand hygiene habits, hands down." Available online. URL: http://www .asm.org/Media/index.asp?bid=38075. Accessed September 21, 2005.

Table 7.4 Rabies vaccines licensed and marketed in the United States, 2005

Product Name	Produced by	Marketed by	For Use In	Dosage (mL)	Age at primary vaccination*	Booster recommended	Route of Inoculation
A) Monovalent (Inactivated)							
Defensor 1	Pfizer, Inc. License No. 189	Pfizer, Inc.	Dogs	1	3 mos.**	Annually	IM[†] or SC[††]
			Cats	1	3 mos.	Annually	SC
Defensor 3	Pfizer, Inc. License No. 189	Pfizer, Inc.	Dogs	1	3 mos.	1 year later and triennially	IM or SC
			Cats	1	3 mos.	1 year later and triennially	SC
			Sheep	2	3 mos.	Annually	IM
			Cattle	2	3 mos.	Annually	IM
Rabdomun	Pfizer, Inc. License No. 189	Schering-Plough	Dogs	1	3 mos.	1 year later and triennially	IM or SC
			Cats	1	3 mos.	1 year later and triennially	SC
			Sheep	2	3 mos.	Annually	IM
			Cattle	2	3 mos.	Annually	IM
Rabdomun 1	Pfizer, Inc. License No. 189	Schering Plough	Dogs	1	3 mos.	Annually	IM or SC
			Cats	1	3 mos.	Annually	SC
Rabvac 1	Fort Dodge Animal Health License No. 112	Fort Dodge Animal Health	Dogs	1	3 mos.	Annually	IM or SC
			Cats	1	3 mos.	Annually	Sc
Rabvac 3	Fort Dodge Animal Health License No. 112	Fort Dodge Animal Health	Dogs	1	3 mos.	1 year later and triennially	IM or SC
			Cats	1	3 mos.	1 year later and triennially	IM or SC
			Horses	2	3 mos.	Annually	IM
Rabvac 3 TF	Fort Dodge Animal Health License No. 112		Dogs	1	3 mos.	1 year later and triennially	IM or Sc
			Cats	1	3 mos.	1 year later and triennially	IM or SC
			Horses	2	3 mos.	Annually	IM

Table 7.4 Rabies vaccines licensed and marketed in the United States, 2005 (continued)

Product Name	Produced by	Marketed by	For Use In	Dosage (mL)	Age at primary vaccination	Booster recommended	Route of Inoculation
Prorab-1	Intervet, Inc. License No. 286	Intervet, Inc.	Dogs	1	3 mos.	Annually	IM or SC
			Cats	1	3 mos.	Annually	IM or SC
			Sheep	2	3 mos.	Annually	IM
Prorab-3TF	Intervet, Inc. License No. 286	Intervet, Inc.	Cats	1	3 mos.	1 year later and triennially	IM or SC
Imrab 3	Merial, Inc. License No. 298	Merial, Inc.	Dogs	1	3 mos.	1 year later and triennially	IM or SC
			Cats	1	3 mos.	1 year later and triennially	IM or SC
			Sheep	2	3 mos.	1 year later and triennially	IM or SC
			Cattle	2	3 mos.	Annually	IM or SC
			Horses	2	3 mos.	Annually	IM or SC
			Ferrets	1	3 mos.	Annually	SC
IMRAB 3 TF	Merial, Inc. License No. 298	Merial, Inc.	Dogs	1	3 mos	1 year later and triennially	IM or SC
			Cats	1	3 mos	1 year later and triennially	IM or SC
			Ferrets	1	3 mos		SC
IMRAB Large Animal	Merial, Inc. License No. 298	Merial, Inc.	Cattle	1	3 mos	Annually	IM or SC
			Horses	2	3 mos	Annually	IM or SC
			Sheep	2	3 mos	Annually	IM or SC
IMRAB 1	Merial, Inc. License No. 298	Merial, Inc.	Dogs	2	3 mos	1 year later and triennially	SC
			Cats	1	3 mos	Annually	Sc

Table 7.4 Rabies vaccines licensed and marketed in the United States, 2005 (continued)

Product Name	Produced by	Marketed by	For Use In	Dosage (mL)	Age at primary vaccination	Booster recommended	Route of Inoculation
B) Monovalent (Rabies glycoprotein, live canary pox vector)							
PURAVAX Feline Rabies	Merial, Inc. License No. 298	Merial, Inc.	Cats	1	8 wks	Annually	SC
C) Combination (Inactivated rabies)							
Equine POTOMAVAC +IMRAB	Merial, Inc. License No. 298	Merial, Inc.	Horses	1	3 mos	Annually	IM
MYSTIQUE II POTOMAVAC +	Intervet, Inc. License No. 288	Intervet, Inc.	Horses	1	3 mos	Annually	IM
D) Combination (Rabies glycoprotein, live canary pox vector)							
PUREVAX Feline 3/Rabies	Merial, Inc. License No. 298	Merial, Inc.	Cats	1	6 wks	Annually	SC
PUREVAX Feline 4/Rabies	Merial, Inc. License No. 298	Merial, Inc.	Cats	1	8 wks	Annually	SC
E) Oral (Rabies glycoprotein, live vaccinia vector) - Restricted to Use in State and Federal Rabies-Control Probrams							
RABORAL V-RG	Merial, Inc. License No. 298	Merial, Inc.	Raccoons Coyotes	N/A	N/A	As determined by local authorities	Oral

* Minimum age (or older) and revaccinated 1 year later

** 1 month=28 days

† Intramuscularly

†† Subcutaneously

evidence of wounds of unknown origin. In addition, contact with humans during this period should be avoided.

CONTROL OF RABIES IN WILDLIFE

Two other types of vaccines, used primarily in wildlife, include oral vaccines and live **recombinant** vaccines. The oral vaccine is placed inside a waxy covering of beef tallow, which acts as

Table 7.5 Rabies Post-exposure Prophylaxiws Guide— United States, 1999

Animal type	Evaluation and disposition of animal	Post-exposure prophylaxis recommendations
Dogs, cats, and ferrets	Healthy and available for 10 days observation	Persons should not begin prophylaxis unless animal develops clinical signs of rabies.*
Rabid or suspected rabid		Immediately vaccinate. Consult public health officials.
Unknown (e.g., escaped)		Consult public health official.
Skunks, raccoons, foxes and most other carnivores, and bats	Regarded as rabid unless animal proven negative by laboratory tests+	Consider immediate vaccination.
Livestock, small rodents, lagomorphs (rabbits and hares), large rodents (woodchucks and beavers), and other mammals	Consider individually.	Consult public health officials. Bites of squirrels, hamsters, guinea pigs, gerbils, chipmunks, rats, mice, other small rodents, rabbits, and hares almost never require antirabies post-exposure prophylaxis.

*   During the 10-day observation period, begin post-exposure prophylaxis at the first sign of rabies in a dog, cat, or ferret that has bitten someone. If the animal exhibits clinical signs of rabies, it should be euthanized immediately and tested.

+   The animal should be euthanized and tested as soon as possible. Holding for observation is not recommended. Discontinue vaccine if immunofluorescence test results of the animal are negative.

Figure 7.2 Bait containing rabies vaccine. Courtesy of Texas Department of State Health Services, Infectious Disease Control Unit

bait. Carnivores, such as foxes, are the targets of these baits. Oral vaccines were developed in the mid-1980s and have been used extensively in southern Ontario. Originally dropping 285,000 baits from airplanes in Ontario in 1989, the number increased each year to a peak of 1.8 million baits delivered in 1995. This approach has successfully broken the red fox rabies cycle in this area of North America. Similar baiting programs are also currently being utilized in Europe with great success.

Live recombinant vaccines are interesting because they involve the use of other types of viruses to help control rabies

Figure 7.3 A little brown bat eats a katydid. © Joe McDonald/Corbis

in wildlife. The word "recombinant" indicates that advanced molecular biology techniques have been employed to excise only the rabies virus G gene (this gene produces the rabies virus glycoprotein—refer back to Figure 2.2) and placed it into the genomic DNA of either the vaccinia virus or the canarypox virus. Because these viruses now express the foreign rabies G gene, in addition to the normal vaccinia or canarypox virus genes, they are said to be recombinant. In addition, these recombinant viruses have not been inactivated, thus we have a "live recombinant vaccine." When bait is eaten, the animal's immune system will develop antibodies against the rabies G protein and protect it against rabies—the vaccinia virus or canarypox virus, also present in the animal's body, is harmless to the animal. These types of recombinant vaccines, made into bait with polymerized dog food or fishmeal (Figure 7.2), are currently being used in New York, New Jersey, Ohio, Vermont, and other states to help break the raccoon rabies cycle.

A CASE STUDY

In 1995, a four-year-old girl was sleeping in her room when her aunt was awakened by sounds coming from the girl's room. A bat was creating the noise, and it was captured, killed, and discarded. During this time, the little girl did not wake up. She reported no bites and none were found when she was examined. One month later she became sick and died of rabies. Subsequent analysis of the bat, which was retrieved from the yard, showed that it was positive for rabies. Can you name all of the things that were not done in this situation?

First and foremost, medical treatment for the girl and her aunt was not sought. This would have included testing the bat for rabies with immediate initiation of PET. The girl's life could probably have been saved if these steps had been followed.

It was not recognized that this bat was behaving abnormally. It was making noises, whereas bats normally like to hide. Bats are great fliers, but this bat was

CONTROL OF RABIES IN BATS—A SPECIAL SITUATION

Can you figure out why control of rabies in bats would be considered a special type of situation? First, think about the vaccines and treatment available for humans. Then, consider what is available to treat your pet. Third, think about the use of recombinant vaccines and how they are being used to target wild animals to reduce or break rabies cycles in areas of North America and Europe. So the question is, are there baits or other treatments available for use with bats? Unfortunately, the answer is no. Most bats (Figure 7.3) either eat insects or fruits, so it would be very difficult to develop effective baits for them.

having trouble flying. The bat's behavior should have been a warning sign that it was sick.

The adults in this case did not realize that bats have very small teeth and their bites can be superficial and completely invisible. Just because the child did not wake up when bitten, does not mean she did not sustain a bite. Children tend to sleep heavily and may not wake up after receiving a very small bite from a bat.

The moral of this sad story is to always seek medical attention if you find a bat in your house. It may even be necessary to close the room where the bat is until a professional can be hired to catch the bat for testing. PET can always be stopped early, but you cannot come back to life for a second chance.

(Source: Centers for Disease Control and Prevention. "Bats & Rabies." Available online. URL: http://www.cdc.gov/ncidod/dvrd/rabies/Bats_&_Rabies/bats&.htm. Updated on December 1, 2003.)

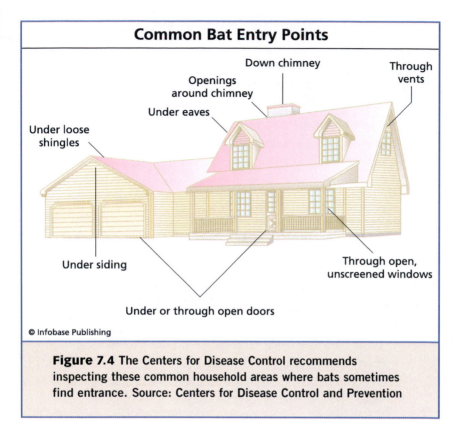

Common Bat Entry Points

Down chimney

Through vents

Openings around chimney

Under eaves

Under loose shingles

Under siding

Through open, unscreened windows

Under or through open doors

© Infobase Publishing

Figure 7.4 The Centers for Disease Control recommends inspecting these common household areas where bats sometimes find entrance. Source: Centers for Disease Control and Prevention

People have many misconceptions about bats, which is too bad because they are very interesting creatures and very important to farmers around the world. Here are a few facts: Most bats do not have rabies; they are not blind; they are not rodents or birds; and they will not suck your blood while you are sleeping. The most important point, however, is that many need our protection since their numbers are declining due to loss of habitat, and this is best accomplished by educating ourselves and others about them.

It is important to keep in mind, though, that most recent cases of human rabies have involved rabies associated with bats. There are a few things you need to do if you come into contact with a bat. If you are bitten or if saliva gets into your eyes or mouth, then you will need to seek medical attention immediately. Most people, however, do not even realize they have been bitten because the teeth of bats are very fine and may not leave an obvious wound. Therefore, if you see a bat in your room or in the room of another family member, then everybody inside the house should seek the advice of a doctor. In addition, it will be important to have the bat tested for rabies. Consider the case study on page 98 and the consequences of not seeking medical care.

Bats should not gain access to rooms in homes. It is a good idea to bat-proof your house to keep them out. Figure 7.4 provides some guidelines on where to concentrate your efforts when bat-proofing a house. Look for any holes in the outer walls that might be access points for bats—all openings larger than a quarter-inch by half-inch should be caulked.[49] Draft guards at the base of doors and screens in windows will also prevent entry. If bats are already present, watch for them to leave at dusk, then loosely hang clear plastic sheeting or fine netting over the opening. They can crawl out easily, but will be unable to reenter. Once they are all gone, the opening can be sealed permanently. Also remember, young bats are born in the summer, so it is best not to exclude the adults until after the offspring are able to fly.

8

The Strange, The Mysterious, and The Tragic

Because rabies has been around at least since the first humans walked the earth and causes those infected to behave in bizarre ways, it is little wonder that strange ideas or myths developed over time. Imagine living in the 18th century, without the knowledge we enjoy today, and watching someone go mad as a result of a bite from a dog or wolf. How do you think you would respond to such an event? They didn't have the Internet to search for medical symptoms and information about treatment; they didn't have drugstores from which to buy medicine; they didn't have cars or easy modes of transportation (many villages were isolated); they didn't even know what was causing the biting victims to die such horrible deaths. This scenario, therefore, may have been how fear, superstition, and hysteria were able to take hold of entire populations of villages. Even today, odd events still happen that are related to rabies—events that may convince observers that something sinister is associated with this ancient disease.

DID RABIES LEAD TO THE VAMPIRE LEGEND?

Bram Stroker's novel *Dracula*, immortalized over one hundred years ago, features the legend of vampires, which is a popular fictional theme in old movies (Figure 8.1) as well as in recent television series, such as *Buffy the Vampire Slayer*. To people in Eastern Europe during the 1700s, however,

Figure 8.1 Max Shreck as Count Orlock in the 1922 silent film *Nosferatu*, a classic and frightening depiction of vampirism. Some characteristics of vampires may have been inspired by rabies victims. © Bettmann/Corbis

vampires were not considered some sort of entertainment, but creatures that were very real and to be feared. In 1693, it was reported that strange cadavers, full of liquid blood, had been taken by the devil.[50] Soon, the belief that the corpses left their graves spread through the Balkan area of Europe.[50] A report from a village in this region stated, "The inhabitants of the village saw a ghost which appeared to some people in the form of a dog, to others in the shape of a gaunt and hideous man, and who was seen not only by one individual but by many, and who caused persons the greatest alarm and torment by assaulting them fiercely, by seizing their throats so that they were almost suffocated. The ghost even attacked animals, and cows were found half dead just as if they had been severely beaten."[50]

According to lore, vampires slept in a grave during the day, but left at dusk to attack victims. They supposedly sucked the blood of their victims, which included people as well as animals. After an attack, the bite victim had only teeth marks as evidence of what had happened. Eventually, there would be a personality change and they would become irrational and aggressive as they turned into a newly transformed vampire. Protective measures against vampire attacks included garlic and crucifixes, burying suspicious corpses on islands or lakes, or pouring water around their coffins.[50] A suspicious cadaver was one that had a good external appearance, a swollen body full of liquid blood that ran out of the mouth, prominent genitalia, and emitted a cry when a wooden stake was driven through the heart.[50] If a vampire was thought to be present in a village, all of the graves in the churchyard were dug up and those corpses that were well preserved or had moved in their grave, had a stake driven through their hearts or were decapitated.[51]

Once rabies enters the body, it targets the nervous system. In particular, the virus has a predilection for the limbic system of the brain, which regulates emotion and behavior. As a result, most human cases result in the furious form of rabies. An untreated person with furious rabies develops restlessness, insomnia, and starts to wander aimlessly (could be a vampire walking at night). Extreme aggression from furious rabies results in ferocious attacks on anyone nearby (vampires attack and bite their victims). A person was not considered to be rabid if he could stand the sight of his own image in a mirror. Hypersensitivity to many stimuli, however, could trigger convulsive spasms of the facial and vocal muscles, such that a rabid person (or a vampire) would be unable to see their image in the mirror—even the sight of the mirror itself could trigger spasms. Odors too could elicit spasms, with one example being the smell of garlic; this was also used to ward off vampire attacks. Likewise, light was another powerful stimulus to rabies victims and could explain why vampires only came out at night. Victims of a bite were transformed into new vampires; similarly, rabies can be transmitted to another person by a bite.

When people are buried, there are predictable changes that occur over time as the body decays, but environmental factors can slow the time line significantly. Such was the case in the Balkan region of Eastern Europe in the 1700s. Preservation of the cadaver can be explained by the coldness of the region—cold temperatures tend to delay decay. The burial of the dead in areas of high humidity turns subcutaneous tissue into a waxy-like substance and allows for corpses to be identified years after they were first interred.[50] Together, these could have led to the appearance of well-preserved cadavers, which provided strong proof of a cadaver being a vampire. The swelling and foul smell of cadavers were due to a specific stage of decomposition where the internal tissues liquify and gases form. Vampires too were not nice, clean creatures, but smelled badly. As gases continued to build up, they caused swelling of body, genitalia, neck, and face, with protrusion of the tongue, and bloody liquid to ooze from the mouth. Vampires sucked blood of their victims, therefore, they were full of blood as were the corpses. Apparently, vampires were sloppy eaters, too, as part of their meal flowed from their mouths. And when stakes were driven into a supposedly well-preserved cadaver, escaping gases made sounds that were attributed to the anguished cry of a doomed vampire.

Dogs or other wild animals could have dug up cadavers, giving the impression that vampires had left their graves. This, along with the fact that both humans and animals exhibit the same bizarre behavior when rabid, resulted in people of that time associating vampires with animals. Perhaps this led to the idea of vampires transmogrifying (changing) into animals, such as bats.

Imagine all of this information filling the minds of uneducated people in the Balkans and other areas of Europe in the 1700s. These same people believed in spirits and ghosts and had no other way to explain bizarre phenomena. It is conceiv-

STRANGE TREATMENTS

Wild notions arose over time concerning the effects of rabies on humans. Proposed treatments for this disease were no exception. In the first century AD, Roman scholar Aulus Cornelius Celsus recommended treating patients by "excising" bitten tissue, cauterizing (burning or searing) the wound with a red-hot iron, and dunking the victim into a pool of water. Later nitric acid was used instead of hot irons. There were no anesthetics or painkillers at that time, so you can imagine the terrible pain and screaming that must have taken place when the hot iron was applied. Interestingly, Louis Pasteur, as a boy, witnessed a villager undergoing the hot iron treatment. It was an image that stayed with him for the rest of his life. Harsh as this treatment sounds, it may have been effective in a few instances at eliminating virus from the wound and preventing development of disease.

Other odd ideas for treating rabies included the Chinese use of musk and cinnabar (natural source of red mercuric sulfide), ducking stools (a device for punishment to which the offender was tied and ducked into water), the plant wormwood, and ashes of seahorses. In New York in 1806, the legislature awarded $1,000 to John M. Crous for developing a "cure" comprised of a tablet made from the pulverized jawbone of a dog, a dried tongue of a newly foaled colt, and corroded copper from an English penny minted during the reign of George I. It was common practice in the early American West to treat animal bites with "madstones," which were gallstones of albino deer or albino cattle.[2]

Figure 8.2 Author Edgar Allan Poe. © Library of Congress

able, therefore, that this is how the vampire legend started, but this is just one possible explanation.

A MYSTERIOUS DEATH

Edgar Allan Poe (Figure 8.2) was an American writer of poetry and short stories. He, more than anyone else, transformed the short story from anecdote to art. Poe was one of the first to write fictional detective stories and tales of the macabre. He was also a literary critic who wrote serious, analytical reviews that earned him respect as a critic. These latter works resulted in universal influence on literature.

Born in 1809, Poe's life was not what you might imagine, based on his fame today. That he had exceptional literary talent was obvious, but he apparently had little ability to endear himself to people, particularly those for whom he worked. Poe's drinking was also a problem to his employers. In addition, his stinging criticisms, while increasing the sales of local magazines, offended many. As a result, he went from job to job trying to establish himself as a literary journalist with only moderate success. The mystery, however, is not his lack of success securing a steady job, but the cause of his death in 1849, which is still controversial today.

In 1849, Poe was on his way to visit his fiancée when he disappeared for three days. He was found in a gutter outside a pub in Baltimore, delirious, trembling, and wearing someone else's clothes. Obviously in need of help, he was taken to a hospital where he lapsed into a coma, awoke, regained rational thought for a short period, and then became delirious again. Poe fought with the medical staff and eventually had to be restrained. He never regained lucid thought long enough to explain what had happened and within a few days, he died. Since it was widely known Poe was an alcoholic as well as an opiate drug user, it was assumed he died as a result of complications of his addictions. A doctor from the University of Maryland recently reviewed the medical case, however, and stated that Poe may have died as a result of rabies and not due to "congestion of the brain," which is the official recorded cause of death.[52]

Delirium can be caused by a variety of problems including trauma, vascular disorders in the brain, epilepsy, or infections. Withdrawal from alcohol was also a possibility, although Poe had abstained from alcohol for six months prior to his death and there was no record of alcohol use when he entered the hospital. Significantly, it is unusual for someone suffering from alcohol withdrawal to become ill, recover for a short period, only to relapse and die.[52] Withdrawal from opiates also did not fit Poe's symptoms.[52]

The final stages of rabies, on the other hand, include periods of confusion and broad swings in pulse rate, respiration, and body temperature, all of which were observed during Poe's stay at the hospital. Poe also had great difficulty swallowing the water given to him.[52] Fear of water, or hydrophobia, is a classic sign of rabies and is additional evidence pointing to rabies as the cause of Poe's demise. In addition, the average time of survival after the onset of symptoms of rabies is four days, which is exactly the length of time Poe survived in the hospital.[52]

So how is it possible that Edgar Allan Poe, the great American writer, could have contracted rabies? Poe was a lover of cats and had several as pets. It is conceivable that one bit him, perhaps as much as a year before, since it is possible to be infected with rabies for extended periods before symptoms actually manifest themselves. Unfortunately, no autopsy was performed and the exact cause of his death will remain a mystery, yet all available evidence points to rabies as the real cause of Poe's death.

TRAGIC ORGAN DONATION

A very unusual event occurred in 2004, in which a patient at a hospital presented with severe mental state fluctuations and fever. Imaging analysis identified bleeding in his brain, which worsened quickly and the patient died.[53] Since he was an organ donor, he was screened by standard procedures to determine if there were any reasons to limit donation of his organs. Lungs, liver, and kidney were subsequently harvested.

While the recipient of the lungs died during the operation, the outcome of the other patients was completely different. The recipient of the liver was a patient with end-stage liver disease with a transplant being his only hope. Initially, he did well and was discharged from the hospital five days after surgery.[53] Twenty-one days following the transplant, the patient was readmitted with tremors, lethargy, and anorexia.[53] His neurological status declined rapidly with subsequent intubation and critical care. MRI (magnetic resonance imaging) analysis revealed encephalitis. The patient continued to deteriorate and he died six days later.

A woman with end-stage kidney disease received the first kidney. Seven days after surgery she went home. Twenty-five days after transplant, she was readmitted with right-side flank pain and underwent an appendectomy.[53] Two days later, she exhibited twitching and lethargy. Imaging analysis initially showed no abnormalities. Within two days she presented with worsening mental status, seizures, and respiratory failure with subsequent intubation.[53] Imaging analysis two weeks after entry into the hospital revealed cerebral edema.[53] The patient died soon after this test.

The second kidney went to a man who also had end-stage kidney disease. He was discharged from the hospital 12 days after surgery. Twenty-seven days later, he went to an emergency room due to spasms and an altered mental state.[53] Imaging again showed no problems.[53] This was followed by continued deterioration of his mental status and eventual respiratory failure with intubation.[53] Ten days later, imaging analysis was repeated and demonstrated the presence of edema in the brain.[53] This transplant patient subsequently died.

In all of the above patients, histological analysis of brain tissue showed the presence of Negri bodies, and they were diagnosed with rabies. These results were confirmed by the direct FAT test. Injection of brain material from one of the patients into mice led to the death of the mice, with subsequent analysis of brain tissue being positive for rabies virus.[53] Serological testing of the donor and all three organ recipients were positive for anti-rabies antibodies. Further analysis of the rabies virus found it was the type associated with bats.[53]

How did these patients become infected with rabies? Since you already know that this virus targets and replicates in neural tissue, the obvious answer is via nerves innervating these organs in the donor. Subsequent transfer of the organs to the recipients resulted in transfer of donor nerve fibers as well. The virus then replicated and made its way to the brain where it caused a fatal disease.

These cases represent the first confirmed transmission of rabies by way of solid organ transplant. They were included in this chapter not to scare you—transmission of any infectious disease during transplantation is extremely rare and the benefits of organ transplantation far outweigh the risks—but to demonstrate to you again how deadly this preventable disease can be. These tragedies could have been avoided if initial organ-screening procedures had included a test for rabies, which was not routinely done. Federal agencies are currently reviewing organ donation procedures and screening practices to determine if changes need to be made.[53]

WEIRD ON A LARGE SCALE

Milk is an item few of us give a second thought to. It is certainly easy enough to go to the store and buy a gallon of cold, fresh milk that is safe to drink. But do you know why it is safe? It is because of a process called pasteurization, which destroys bacteria and viruses that might otherwise cause illness. It is named after Louis Pasteur, who produced the first rabies vaccine. But what about unpasteurized milk, is it safe to drink? The following two incidents help illustrate why it is not wise to drink unpasteurized milk.

On November 12, 1996, a Jersey dairy cow was diagnosed with rabies by tests conducted on brain tissue by the Massachusetts Department of Health. The rabies virus was the type found to be associated with raccoons. This 14-year-old cow became sick on November 6 and was euthanized on November 10. In an investigation, it was discovered that the cow had been milked between October 26 and November 2. State officials also identified 14 persons who had drank unpasteurized milk collected from this cow.[54] All 14 individuals plus four more dairy workers exposed to saliva from the sick cow were given post-exposure treatment (PET).[54]

On November 12, 1998, a six-year-old Holstein dairy cow was diagnosed with rabies using the direct FAT assay on brain tissue by the Massachusetts Department of Health. The type of rabies was found to be the variant associated with raccoons. There was an initial loss of appetite noted on November 4, with development of hypersalivation on November 6. At first, intestinal obstruction was suspected, but the cow lost coordination, became aggressive, and died on November 8.[54] With the confirmation of rabies, state health officials launched an investigation and found the cow had been milked 12 times the week before it died.[54] They also identified 66 persons who consumed unpasteurized milk from this dairy as well as five dairy employees exposed to the cow's saliva. All persons were given PET.

In neither case had milk or mammary tissue from the cows been collected so that they could have been tested for rabies virus. This testing would have helped to determine the risk of exposure since transmission of rabies virus via unpasteurized milk is theoretically possible.[54] It was this very small chance of infection of large numbers of people that prompted state health officials to err on the side of safety.

SURVIVAL OF CLINICAL RABIES

In September of 2004, a 15-year-old girl was attending church when she noticed a bat on the floor. She picked it up and released it outside. It was never captured for testing and nobody else touched the bat. Before being set free, the bat bit her on the left index finger. The wound was cleaned with hydrogen peroxide, medical attention was not sought, and PET was not administered.[55]

A month later, she presented with fatigue and a tingling and numbness of the left hand. Two days later the girl developed double vision and felt unsteady. This was followed by nausea and vomiting. A pediatrician referred her to a neurologist, who performed image analysis of her brain. Results of these tests were normal. The fourth day after onset of illness, the girl was admitted to a local hospital, where a lumbar puncture was performed. She continued to decline, developing slurred speech, tremors of the left arm, lethargy, and a temperature of 102°F.[55] When the medical staff finally learned of the bat bite (sixth day after onset of illness), they tested the collected cerebral spinal fluid, blood serum, skin samples, and saliva for rabies. While the cerebral spinal fluid and serum were positive for anti-rabies antibodies, the skin and saliva were negative for rabies virus.

The girl was intubated and placed on a ventilator. Additional care included a drug-induced coma as a neuroprotective measure as well as treatment with anti-viral drugs.[55] Lumbar puncture after eight days in a comatose state showed increasing amounts of rabies antibody.[55] She was gradually tapered off of the coma medications, which allowed her to become increasingly alert.[55] On the 36th day of illness, she was transferred to a rehabilitation unit where she continued to improve. By mid-December, the girl was regaining the ability to talk, walk with assistance, feed herself soft foods, use sign language, and solve math problems.[55] Five months after her hospitalization, she was still alert, but had difficulty articulating words, and exhibited uncontrollable movements and an unsteady gait.[56]

This was the first documented case of a person surviving a rabies infection once clinical symptoms appeared. The patient in this case received no pre- or post-exposure treatment. There had been five other people who had survived after onset of illness, but had either been previously vaccinated or received PET. The reasons for the girl's recovery are unknown and rabies should still not be looked upon as a curable disease. Indeed, historically, the mortality rate has been 100 percent once symptoms appear. Therefore, this young girl is extremely lucky.

9

A Final Word

Rabies was once intensely studied by many top research scientists. Today, while still being studied, it has been replaced in terms of importance and sense of urgency with a number of highly visible viruses including HIV (human immunodeficiency virus), SARS (severe acute respiratory syndrome), and influenza. The question is, therefore, what does the future hold for rabies? You might be surprised to learn that rabies is being used as a tool to aid researchers in their study of the human brain. It is also being used as a **vector** or transporter to carry foreign genes into other hosts to obtain an enhanced immune response to other viruses, and studied to develop more stable and effective vaccines for use in third world countries. Obviously, this is not the end of the road for the rabies virus. Only time will tell if it will play a key role in keeping us all healthier in the future.

REVERSE GENETICS: DEVELOPING NOVEL VACCINES AGAINST RABIES

What is reverse genetics? First, consider that we are talking about a virus with a RNA genome. Therefore, reverse genetics in this case means using the rabies virus genomic RNA as a template to make a DNA copy (called copy DNA or cDNA). In Chapter 6, we mentioned an enzyme called reverse transcriptase, which uses RNA as a template to make cDNA. For the simplest case of reverse genetics of rabies, this means making a cDNA of the genomic RNA, and then introducing the cDNA into cells to obtain newly formed progeny virions. The "reverse genetics" part of this process is the production of new virus particles from DNA. Turning the rabies virus RNA into DNA is important because DNA is much more stable than RNA (i.e. RNA degrades faster than DNA) and easier to manipulate. For example, specific sites within the cDNA can be mutated, portions can be deleted, and foreign DNA can be inserted at various sites—none of which can be done with RNA.

One study used the cDNA itself as a DNA rabies vaccine, with the goal of generating a more potent vaccine for dogs using fewer doses. Researchers injected cDNA from a vaccine strain of rabies virus intradermally into the ears of dogs and found that a single dose generated longer lasting immunity to rabies than vaccination done intramuscularly in the leg or intradermally on the back.[57] Field trials on dogs in Tunisia resulted in a stronger induction of anti-rabies antibodies when a DNA rabies vaccine was used (via ear inoculation) in comparison to standard tissue-culture-derived vaccine.[58] These studies thus demonstrate the potential usefulness of DNA rabies vaccines in third-world countries. Also keep in mind that DNA vaccines can be stored at a wider range of temperatures than RNA-based vaccines, another important factor in these countries.

Another current topic of research is the generation of more effective rabies vaccines. Use of oral vaccines in foxes in Europe reduced or eradicated rabies from several countries and clearly demonstrated the effectiveness of this approach. Foxes are the only rabies reservoir in Europe, though, unlike the United States, where multiple species are known reservoirs of rabies, each with their own distinct variants. Therefore, it is necessary to develop vaccines for each variant since a single oral vaccine to one variant may not produce protective immunity in another species of wild animal. Scientists are now using rabies cDNA from vaccine strains of rabies to generate potent oral vaccines specific for a particular variant. This is done by removing the G or glycoprotein gene of the vaccine strain and

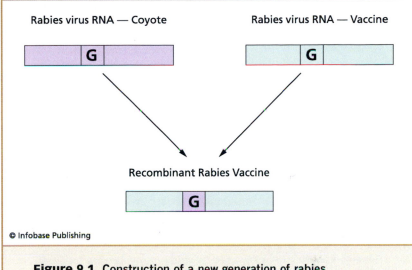

Rabies virus RNA — Coyote

Rabies virus RNA — Vaccine

G

G

Recombinant Rabies Vaccine

G

© Infobase Publishing

Figure 9.1 Construction of a new generation of rabies vaccines to be used in wild animals. The G gene is removed from a vaccine strain of rabies (right) and is replaced with the G gene from a rabies variant from a wild animal, such as a coyote (left). The end result is a recombinant vaccine strain of rabies that contains the G gene from the coyote variant (center, bottom). Such recombinants can easily be constructed for other rabies variants in the hope of creating more effective vaccines. **Source: Thomas Kienzle.**

replacing it with the G gene from the target rabies variant, such as a coyote. Thus, this altered cDNA can now be used to generate new virus particles whose genome carries the G gene from the coyote variant, which can in turn be used in oral vaccines for coyotes.[59] (Figure 9.1). Do you know why the G gene was chosen for study? It is because the rabies glycoprotein is the main target of the host immune system, such that if there is a strong enough immune response to the rabies glycoprotein, then clinical disease can be prevented. Therefore, species-specific G proteins may provide the best chance at developing an improved vaccine.

An intriguing twist on the use of the rabies G gene for the development of better rabies vaccines involves the use of tobacco plants. In this research, the G gene from rabies cDNA was removed and placed into tobacco plants, thus generating **transgenic** tobacco plants.[60] These plants synthesized the rabies G glycoprotein in their leaves.[60] When the G glycoprotein was purified from the tobacco leaves and used to vaccinate mice, a strong immune response to the G protein protected

SPANISH FLU RECONSTRUCTED—WHAT IS YOUR OPINION?

Reverse genetics is being used to study many viruses today. In 2005, scientists used this powerful technique to reconstruct the infamous virus responsible for the 1918 Spanish influenza pandemic. This was the most devastating influenza outbreak in history because it killed between 20 and 50 million people worldwide. As soldiers returned home following World War I, they facilitated spread of the virus to the United States and other countries. Within a few years, this particular virus disappeared and has not been seen since, until 2005, that is. Scientists purified viral RNA from a victim frozen in permafrost in 1918, as well as RNA obtained from archived lung tissue. Influenza is a RNA virus whose genome is segmented; therefore, it was necessary to turn each of the eight viral RNA segments into DNA (reverse transcription). Each DNA segment was then introduced into cells grown in culture, resulting in progeny 1918 Spanish influenza.

The goal of such research was to try to learn why this particular virus was so deadly and, hopefully, to recognize characteristics of possible future pandemic influenza viruses. To date, scientists have learned it is more pathogenic (ability to cause disease) than other influenza viruses. It can grow in cultured cells without special enzymes (other influenza them against intracerebral **lethal challenge** using wild type rabies virus.[60] Such studies show that plants may represent a future method of generating vaccines.[60]

REVERSE GENETICS: USE OF RABIES VIRUS AS A VECTOR

A different use of reverse genetics has allowed scientists to develop rabies virus as a vector, where it is used to carry a foreign gene from another virus into a host with the purpose of

viruses need an enzyme called trypsin to gain entry into cultured cells), is 100 times more lethal in mice than other influenza viruses, kills 10-day-old embryonated eggs, and shows enhanced growth in cultured human lung cells. These data indicate that this virus had extraordinary virulence.

Should scientists have reconstructed such a deadly virus, one that hasn't been seen in nature since the 1918 pandemic? This research comes in the middle of a current pandemic scare: the avian influenza H5N1 is presently spreading around the globe in birds but has not yet been found to infect humans easily. On one hand, research may help in predicting, preventing, and treating future pandemics, but on the other hand, it would be devastating if such a deadly virus were to be accidentally released. What is your opinion? Should the researchers have recreated the 1918 influenza virus? You may want to consider such factors as there being a higher world population today than in 1918, current ease of global travel, and the availability of antivirals and vaccines today that were not available in 1918.

Source: Tumpey, T. M., et al., *Science* 310 (2005): 77-80; Tumpey, T. M., et al., *Journal of Virology* 79 (2005): 14933-14944.

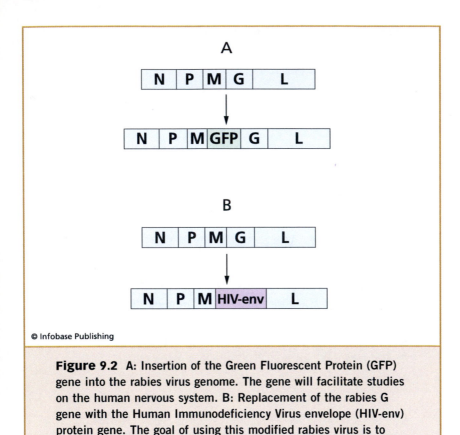

A

B

Figure 9.2 **A:** Insertion of the Green Fluorescent Protein (GFP) gene into the rabies virus genome. The gene will facilitate studies on the human nervous system. **B:** Replacement of the rabies G gene with the Human Immunodeficiency Virus envelope (HIV-env) protein gene. The goal of using this modified rabies virus is to generate a strong immune response to HIV that will protect against clinical disease. Source: Thomas Kienzle.

initiating a strong immune response to the foreign gene product or for using the modified virus as a way to study the central nervous system (see below). This is done by inserting a foreign gene into the rabies RNA genome (Figure 9.2A), which results in expression of the foreign protein. A second way this can be done is to remove the rabies G gene and replace it with a glycoprotein gene from another virus (Figure 9.2B). Since the surface glycoprotein determines which cells the virus will infect (you already know this from Chapter 2), a new surface protein will recognize different cellular receptor molecules with the rabies virus infecting different cells. In each case, the modified rabies virus is called a recombinant virus.

One example is the use of rabies as a vaccine against HIV (human immunodeficiency virus), which causes AIDS. Rabies viruses stably expressing HIV proteins have been constructed and were able to induce potent immune responses to HIV.[61] Scientists are also trying to develop rabies-based vaccines that express two HIV proteins instead of one. Are the immune responses sufficient to protect against disease? Unfortunately, this has not yet been accomplished, but it is the goal of many research laboratories around the country. HIV is not the only virus being targeted by scientists using rabies-based vaccines. Others include influenza virus, hepatitis C virus, respiratory syncytial virus, papillomavirus, and the SARS virus.[61]

TARGETING CANCER

Some viruses kill the cells they infect, while others, such as rabies virus, do not. Scientists have taken advantage of viruses that have a lytic (i.e. killing) life cycle. Researchers are using vesicular stomatitis virus, another member of the Rhabdoviridae family that kills the cells it infects, to target specific types of cancer. While this virus causes disease in animals, it is mostly non-pathogenic in humans. Significantly, this virus replicates almost exclusively in cancer cells and by doing so kills the cancer cells. Like rabies virus, recombinant vesicular stomatitis viruses can be generated to direct the altered viruses to cancer cells. Vesicular stomatitis virus has now been shown to be an efficient killer of several kinds of cancers including malignant glioma, melanoma, hepatocellular carcinoma, breast adenocarcinoma, some leukemias, and tumors arising from prostate cancer.[62]

RABIES AND BRAIN CONNECTIONS

The nerve highway within human brains is quite complex and, for the most part, is still a mystery to scientists. One tool for unraveling its secrets is the use of live, recombinant rabies virus to map the flow of information within the central nervous system. Such viruses have been designated as transneuronal tracers. "Trans" means the viruses travel from one nerve to another. "Neuronal" means these viruses only infect nerve cells. The term "tracers" is used because the rabies virus has been modified to carry a foreign gene that allows scientists to follow its movement from the point of injection in a muscle, to the brain, and then within the brain as the virus replicates. One gene that has been inserted into the rabies virus genome is the Green Fluorescent Protein (GFP) gene and when it is expressed, it fluoresces a bright green color at a certain wavelength when examined under a fluorescent microscope.[63] Another advantage of using live viruses is that their numbers increase as they replicate and, hence, the amount of GFP also increases within the brain. Rabies is the most effective virus for these studies as it infects almost exclusively **motor neurons**, the nerve cells that supply motor function, after injection into a muscle.[63]

Another way to study brain circuitry is the simple use of rabies virus that has not been genetically altered. This would be done by injection of the virus into a muscle, then at some predetermined time later, harvesting the brain, generating thin sections, and using an anti-rabies antibody to map areas of the brain to which the virus had traveled. This type of work, of course, cannot be done in humans, but only in animals, such as mice or non-human primates. The information learned from research on animals, however, could one day be used to treat central nervous system diseases in humans. Interestingly, one laboratory is currently using rabies viruses to determine the precise nerve cells involved in emotional behavior in primates.[64] Cutting-edge research such as this is becoming more and more common as scientists slowly but surely decipher the mysteries of the human brain.

THE REAL FINAL WORD

What does the future hold for you? Do you already know what career is the right one for you? Perhaps you will become a scientist and study viruses or a medical doctor specializing in infectious diseases. Perhaps you will develop the dream of helping third world countries to finally eradicate rabies—a disease that is totally preventable with the appropriate vaccines and treatment, yet still causes significant mortality. Will you be the person who finally develops a potent, longer lasting vaccine that can be used to immunize dogs in a single dose, in areas where dog rabies is still endemic? This will involve hard work both in the laboratory and in the field—it won't be easy, particularly when you consider the work will have to be done in a number of foreign countries that don't have the same infrastructure as we have here in the United States. But think about the lives you could save—most rabies deaths in third world countries occur in children. Maybe one of the children you save would grow up to be a president, a world-renowned musician, or a Nobel prize winner for developing a cure for a disease such as malaria. Attaining such a goal will take courage, skill, and, most of all, a great desire to succeed.

Notes

1. Gomez-Alonso, J. "Rabies: a possible explanation for the vampire legend." *Historical Neurology* 51 (1998): 856–859.

2. Kaplan, M. M., and H. Koprowski. "Rabies." *Scientific American* 242 (1980): 120–134.

3. Baer, G.M. "Rabies Virus." In: *Virology*, B.N. Fields, ed. New York, NY: Raven Press, 1985.

4. Ludwig, B., F. B. Kraus, R. Allwinn, H. W. Doerr, and W. Preiser. "Viral zoonoses — a threat under control?" *Intervirology* 46 (2003): 71–78.

5. Krebs, J. W., E. J. Mandel, D. L. Swerdlow, and C. E. Rupprecht. "Rabies surveillance in the United States during 2003." *Journal of the American Veterinary Medical Association* 225 (2004): 1837–1849.

6. World Health Organization. "Epidemiology." Available online. URL: http://www.who.int/rabies/epidemiology/en/.

7. Shope, R., and R. Tesh. "The ecology of rhabdoviruses that infect invertebrates." In: *The Rhabdoviruses*, R. Wagner, ed. New York, NY: Plenum, 1987.

8. Jackson, A., R. Francki, and D. Zuidema. "Biology, structure, and replication of plant rhabdoviruses." In: *The Rhabdoviruses*, R. Wagner, ed. New York, NY: Plenum, 1987.

9. Schmitt, B. "Vesicular Stomatitis." *Veterinary and Clinical North American Food Animal Practice* 18 (2002): 453–459.

10. The Comptroller and Auditor General, National Audit Office. "The 2001 Outbreak of Foot and Mouth Disease." Available online. URL: http://www.nao.gov.uk/pn/01–02/0102939.htm. Posted June 21, 2002.

11. de Mattos, C. .A., C. C. de Mattos, and C. E. Rupprecht. "Rhabdoviruses." In: *Fields Virology*, D. M. Knipe and P. M. Howley, eds. Philadelphia, PA: Lippincott Williams & Wilkins, 2001.

12. Tordo, N., O. Poch, A. Ermine, G. Keith, and F. Rougeon. "Walking along the rabies genome: is the large G-L intergenic region a remnant gene?" *Proceedings of the National Academy of Science* USA 83 (1986): 3914–3918.

13. Gastka, M., J. Horvath, and T. L. Lentz. "Rabies virus binding to the nicotinic acetylcholine receptor alpha subunit demonstrated by virus overlay protein binding assay." *Journal of General Virology* 77 (1996): 2437–2440.

14. Thoulouze, M. I., M. Lafage, M. Schachner, et al. "The neural cell adhesion molecule is a receptor for rabies virus." *Journal of Virology* 72 (1998): 7181–7190.

15. Tuffereau, C., J. Benejean, A. M. Alfonso, et al. "Neuronal cell surface molecules mediate specific binding to rabies virus glycoprotein expressed by a recombinant baculovirus on the surfaces of lepidopteran cells." *Journal of Virology* 72 (1998): 1085–1091.

16. Rigaut, K. D., D. E. Birk, and J. Lenard. "Intracellular distribution of input vesicular stomatitis virus proteins after uncoating." *Journal of Virology* 65 (1991): 2622–2628.

17. Pattnaik A. K., L. Hwang, T. Li, et al. "Phosphorylation within the amino-terminal acidic domain I of the phosphoprotein of vesicular stomatitis virus is required for transcription but not for replication." *Journal of Virology* 71 (1997): 8167–8175.

18. Mebatsion, T., F. Weiland, and K. K. Conzelmann. "Matrix protein of rabies virus is responsible for the assembly and budding of bullet-shaped particles and interacts with the transmembrane spike glycoprotein G." *Journal of Virology* 73 (1999): 242–250.

19. Hatwick, M.A.W. "Human rabies." *Public Health Review* 3 (1974): 229–274.

20. Charlton, K. M., S. Nadin-Davis, G. A. Casey, et al. "The long incubation period in rabies: delayed progression of infection in muscle cells at the site of

exposure." *Acta Neuropathologica (Berl.)* 94 (1997): 73–77.

21. Ugolini, G. "Specificity of rabies virus as a transneuronal tracer of motor networks: transfer from hypoglossal motorneurons to connected second-order and higher order central nervous system cell groups." *Journal of Comparative Neurology* 356 (1995): 457–480.

22. Baer, G. M., T. R. Shanthaveerappa, and G. H. Bourne. "Studies on the pathogenesis of fixed rabies virus in rats." *Bulletin WHO* 33 (1965): 119–125.

23. Hurst, E. W., and J. L. Pawan. "An outbreak of rabies in Trinidad." *Lancet* 2 (1931): 622–628.

24. Fekadu, M. "Canine rabies." In: *The Natural History of Rabies,* G. M. Baer, ed. Boca Raton, FL: CRC Press Inc., 1991.

25. Doege, T. C., and R. L. Northrop. "Evidence for inapparent rabies infection."*Lancet* ii (1974): 826–829.

26. Green, S. L., L. L. Smith, W. Vernau, and S. M. Beacock. "Rabies in horses: 21 cases (1970–1990)." *Journal of the American Veterinary Medical Association* 200 (1992): 1133–1137.

27. Hudson, L. C., D. Weinstock, T. Jordan, and N. O. Bold-Fletcher. "Clinical features of experimentally induced rabies in cattle and sheep." *Zentralblatt fur Veterinarmedizin. Reihe B* 43 (1996): 85–95.

28. Voros, K., J. Tanyi, and F. Karsai. "Clinical experiences with rabies in cattle in Hungary." *Deutsche Tierarztliche Wochenschrift* 106 (1999): 46–49.

29. Sawyer, W. A., J. H. Bauer, and L. Whitman. "The distribution of yellow fever immunity in North America, Central America, the West Indies, Europe, Asia and Australia, with special reference to the specificity of the protection test." *American Journal of Tropical Medicine* 17 (1937): 137–161.

30. Isakbaeva, E. T., M-A. Widdowson, R. S. Beard, S. N. Bulens, J. Mullins, S. S. Monroe, J. Bresee, P. Sassano, E. H. Cramer, and R. I. Glass. "Norovirus Transmission on Cruise Ship." *Emerging Infectious Diseases* 11 (2005): 154–157.

31. Le Menach, A., J. Legrand, R. F. Grais, C. Viboud, A. J. Valleron, and A. Flahault. "Modeling spatial and temporal transmission of foot-and-mouth disease in France: identification of high-risk areas." *The Veterinary Record* 36 (2005): 699–712.

32. Smith, J. S., L. A. Orciari, and P. A. Yager. "Molecular epidemiology of rabies in the United States." *Seminars in Virology* 6 (1995): 387–400.

33. Messenger, S. L., J. S. Smith, and C. E. Rupprecht. "Emerging epidemiology of bat-associated cryptic cases of rabies in humans in the United States." *Clinical and Infectious Diseases* 35 (2002): 738–747.

34. Jenkins, S. R., B. D. Perry, and W. G. Winkler. "Ecology and epidemiology of raccoon rabies." *Review of Infectious Diseases* 10 (1988): S260–S625.

35. Krebs, J. W., E. J. Mandel, D. L. Swerdlow, and C. E. Rupprecht. "Rabies surveillance in the United States during 2003." *Journal of the American Veterinary Medical Association* 225 (2004): 1837–1849.

36. Messenger, S. L., J. S. Smith, L. A. Orciari, P. A. Yager, and C. E. Rupprecht. "Emerging patthern of rabies deaths and increased viral infectivity." *Emerging Infectious Diseases* 9 (2003): 151–154.

37. Cliquet, F., and E. Picard-Meyer. "Rabies and rabies-related viruses: a modern perspective on an ancient disease." *Revue Scientifique et Technique [International Office of Epizootics]* 23 (2004): 625–642.

38. Cleaveland, S., M. Kaare, P. Tiringa, T. Mlengeya, and J. Barrat. "A dog rabies vaccination campaign in rural Africa: impact on the incidence of dog rabies and human dog-bite injuries." *Vaccine* 21 (2003): 1965–1973.

Notes

39. Cleaveland, S., E. M. Fèvre, M. Kaare, and P. G. Coleman. "Estimating human rabies mortality in the United Republic of Tanzania from dog bite injuries." *Bulletin of the World Health Organization* 80 (2002): 304–310.

40. Fraser, G. C., P. T. Hooper, R. A. Lunt, et al. "Encephalitis caused by a lyssavirus in fruit bats in Australia." *Emerging Infectious Diseases* 2 (1996): 327–331.

41. Blenden, D. C., W. Creech, and M. J. Torres-Anjel. "Use of immunofluorescence examinations of detect rabies virus antigen in the skin of humans with clinical encephalitis." *Journal of Infectious Diseases* 154 (1986): 698–701.

42. Blenden, D. C., J. F. Bell, A. T. Tsao, and J. U. Umoh. "Immunofluorescent examination of the skin of rabies infected animals as a means of early detection of rabies virus antigen to detect rabies." *Journal of Clinical Microbiology* 18 (1983): 1–6.

43. Mathuranayagan, D., and P. V. Rao. "Antemortem diagnosis of human rabies by corneal impression smears using immunofluorescent technique." *Indian Journal of Medical Research* 79 (1984): 463–467.

44. Li, Z., Z. Feng, and H. Ye. "Rabies viral antigen in human tongues and salivary glands." *Journal of Tropical Medicine and Hygiene* 98 (1995): 330332.

45. Kasempimolporn, S., W. Saengseesom, B. Lumlertdacha, and V. Sitprija. "Detection of rabies virus antigen in dog saliva using a latex agglutination test." *Journal of Clinical Microbiology* 38 (2000): 3098–3099.

46. World Health Organization. "Strategies for the control and elimination of rabies in Asia. Report of a WHO inter-regional consultation." Geneva: 2002.

47. Coleman, P. G., E. M. Fèvre, and S. Cleaveland. "Estimating the public health impact of rabies." *Emerging Infectious Diseases* 10 (2004): 140–142.

48. Bogel, K., and F-X. Meslin. "Economics of human and canine rabies elimination: guidelines for programme orientation." *Bulletin of the World Health Organization* 68 (1990): 281–291.

49. Centers for Disease Control and Prevention. "Bats and Rabies." Available online. URL: http://www.cdc.gov/ncidod/dvrd/rabies/Bats_&_Rabies/bats&.htm. Updated December 1, 2003.

50. Gómez-Alonso, J. "Rabies a possible explanation for the vampire legend." *Neurology* 51 (1998): 856–859.

51. Heick, A. "Prince Dracula, rabies, and the vampire legend." *Annals of Internal Medicine* 117(1992): 172–173.

52. Benitez, R. M. "Edgar Allan Poe Mystery." University of Maryland Medical Center on the Web. Available online. URL: http://www.umm.edu/news/releases/news-releases-17.html. Posted September 24, 1996.

53. Centers for Disease Control and Prevention. "Investigation of rabies infections in organ donor and transplant recipients Alabama, Arkansas, Oklahoma, and Texas, 2004." *Mortality and Morbidity Weekly Report* 53 (2004): 586–589.

54. Centers for Disease Control and Prevention. "Mass treatment of humans who drank unpasteurized milk from rabid cows Massachusetts, 1996–1998." *Mortality and Morbidity Weekly Report* 48 (1999): 228–229.

55. Centers for Disease Control and Prevention. "Recovery of a patient from clinical rabies – Wisconsin, 2004." *Mortality and Morbidity Weekly Report* 53 (2004): 1171–1173.

56. Willoughby Jr., C. E., Tieves, K. S., Hoffman, G. M., at el. "Survival after treatment of rabies with induction of coma." *New England Journal of Medicine* 352 (2005): 2508–2514.

57. Lodmell, D. L., M. J. Parnell, J. T. Weyhrich, and L. C. Ewalt. "Canine rabies DNA vaccination: a single-dose

intradermal injection into ear pinnae elicits elevated and persistent levels of neutralizing antibody." *Vaccine* 21 (2003): 3998–4002.

58. Baloul, C., D. Taieb, M. F. Diouani, S. B. Ahmed, Y, Chtourou, et al. "Field trials of a very potent rabies DNA vaccine which induced long lasting virus neutralizing antibodies and protection in dogs in experimental conditions." *Vaccine* September 21 (2005): 1063–1027.

59. Dietzschold, B. "Generation of novel recombinant rabies virus vaccines." Abstract of funded grant from CRISP (computer retrieval of information on scientific projects). Available online. URL: http://crisp.cit.nih.gov/.

60. Ashraf, S., P. K. Singh, D. K. Yadav, M. Shahnawaz, et al. "High level expression of surface glycoprotein of rabies virus in tobacco leaves and its immunoprotective activity in mice." *Journal of Biotechnology* 119 (2005): 1–14.

61. McKenna, P. M., J. P. McGettigan, R. J. Pomerantz, B. Dietzschold, and M. J. Schnell. "Recombinant Rhabdoviruses as potential vaccines for HIV-1 and other diseases." *Current HIV Research* 1 (2003): 229–237.

62. Barber, G. N. "Vesicular stomatitis virus as an oncolytic vector." *Viral Immunology* 17 (2004): 516–527.

63. Morcuende, S., Delgado-Garcia, J., and G. Ugolini. "Neruonal premotor networks involved in eyelid responses: retrograde transneuronal tracing with rabies virus from the orbicularis oculi muscle in the rat." *The Journal of Neuroscience* 22 (2002): 8808–8818.

64. Stefanacci, L. "Defining the multisynaptic circuitry of the amygdala." Abstract of funded grant from CRISP (computer retrieval of information on scientific projects). Available online. URL: http://crisp.cit.nih.gov/.

Glossary

adsorption—Attachment of a virus to its receptor on the cell membrane of the host cell.

antibody (pl. antibodies)—A protein produced in response to an invasion of the body by a pathogen such as a virus or bacterium. Antibodies are found in the blood and are part of the immune system that defends the body against disease.

antigen—A foreign substance, such as a virus or bacterium, that causes an immune response (i.e. activates the body's immune system) when it enters the body. Antigens are recognized by a component of the immune system known as antibodies. Attachment of an antibody to an antigen results in the destruction of the antigen.

assembly—The combining of individual replication units to form progeny virions.

blood-brain barrier—Specialized structure of blood vessels that restrict passage of substances from the blood into the brain.

budding—Process of maturation and release of progeny-enveloped viruses from host cells. This is accomplished when the viral RNP migrates to areas of the cell membrane containing matrix and surface proteins and is covered with the host membrane.

chromophore—The part or chemical group of a molecule that absorbs light over a range of wavelengths.

CNS—Abbreviation for central nervous system, composed of the brain and spinal cord.

condensation—Packaging of the viral RNP into a tightly wrapped structure.

cytology—The branch of biology dealing with the structure, function, pathology, and formation of cells.

cytoplasm—The organized complex of substances and structures of a cell located outside the nucleus. Includes membranes and organelles (e.g., endoplasmic reticulum, mitochondria).

DNA—An abbreviation for deoxyribonucleic acid. DNA is one of the molecules that contains a virus' genetic information. It is made up of long chains of deoxyribonucleotides joined by hydrogen bonds between complementary bases: adenine and thymine or guanine and cytosine.

embryonated egg—A fertilized chicken egg with a living, developing embryo. Embryos usually between seven and 13 days old are best for growing viruses.

encephalitis—Inflammation of the brain, usually due to a viral infection. Involvement of the spinal cord as well is called encephalomyelitis.

endemic—This term describes a disease that persists in a particular region or human population group over a long period of time without reintroduction from the outside.

endocytosis—Uptake of a virus by a cell in which the cell membrane invaginates to form a membrane-bound vesicle with virus particles on the inside. Typically, the term receptor-mediated endocytosis is used to describe the uptake of viruses.

endoplasmic reticulum—Membrane system within the cytoplasm of cells involved in synthesis, modification, and trafficking of proteins.

enzootic—Same as endemic, but refers to populations of animals, not humans.

enzyme—A protein produced by living cells that modifies the rate of chemical reactions but is not used up in the reaction.

epidemic—Major increase in disease incidence over endemic baseline levels affecting either a large number of humans or spreading over a large area. The size of the increase used to determine an epidemic is arbitrary and varies upon the clinical severity, potential economic impact, background infection rate (endemic baseline), and sickness rate.

epizootic—Same as epidemic, but refers to populations of animals, not humans.

formalin—A fixative or preservative used widely in histology laboratories.

frugivorous bats—Bats whose diet is mainly fruit.

grand mal—Severe seizures with spasms involving the whole body and loss of consciousness.

haematophagous bats—Bats whose diet is mostly blood.

hematology—The study of all aspects of blood and blood-forming organs.

histology—A branch of anatomy involved in the study of the microscopic structure of animal or plant tissues.

histopathology—A branch of pathology concerned with the changes in tissue characteristic for a diseased state.

host range—Range of species that can be infected by a particular virus.

Glossary

hygiene—The science of the establishment of health and prevention of disease.

inclusion body—Intracellular structures in cells infected by some viruses that become visible with certain stains. Depending on the virus, these characteristic changes may be found in the nucleus or the cytoplasm. An example of inclusion bodies is Negri bodies found in some rabies-infected cells.

inoculum—Amount of virus introduced into a particular site, such as the site of a dog bite.

insectivorous bats—Bats whose diet is mainly insects.

intracytoplasmic—Located in the cytoplasm of a cell as opposed to intranuclear.

intraspecific—Within a species.

larynx—Voicebox.

latent—Also latency. State of non-replication or dormancy. This occurs with some herpes viruses in central nervous system tissue; for example, there is no HSV-1 virus replication during latency, but upon receipt of an appropriate trigger, the virus replicates and travels down nerves in the face to cause the infamous cold sore.

lethal challenge—Exposure of a laboratory animal to an amount of wild type virus known to be lethal to unvaccinated subjects.

metabolically inert—A dormant state or lacking biological activity.

motor neuron—Nerve cell in the brain involved in movement (in contrast to a sensory neuron).

mRNA—Abbreviation for messenger RNA. mRNAs are also called transcripts. They contain the information for synthesis of a protein, and some mRNAs carry the information for more than one protein.

mutation—A change in the genetic information of an organism.

necropsy—A post-mortem exam done on animals, same as an autopsy done on humans.

Negri bodies—See INCLUSION BODY.

obligate intracellular parasite—A parasite that is completely dependent upon cells for its replication.

passive transport—Movement of substances without using energy.

pathologist—Scientist that focuses on the structural and functional changes due to disease.

phosphorylation—The process of adding phosphate groups (PO_4) to a protein. May be required for enzymatic activity.

photophobia—An abnormal intolerance to light.

polymerase—An enzyme that catalyzes the synthesis of new DNA or RNA using an existing DNA or RNA chain as a template.

prodrome—An early or premonitory stage of disease, often with non-specific symptoms.

protozoology—Zoological branch dealing with the study of single-celled, microscopic organisms called protozoans.

rabies immunoglobulin (RIG)—A solution of blood proteins from a human donor who has received a rabies vaccine and has high levels of anti-rabies antibody in his or her blood. Given as part of PET to provide immediate anti-rabies antibodies until the victims begin to make their own antibodies. RIG are short-lived, with a half-life of about 21 days.

receptor—A molecule on a cell membrane with which a specific substance (such as a hormone) combines to initiate changes in cell function. Viruses also recognize the same receptors and use them to gain entry into cells.

recombinant—A cell, virus, plant, or other organism artificially constructed with new genetic material not found in the original.

replication—Duplication of viral genomic RNA or DNA.

reservoir—Any species of animal that serves as a natural ongoing source of a virus; for example, bats, dogs, and raccoons all serve as reservoirs for the rabies virus; a host.

ribonucleoprotein complex (RNP)—Viral genetic material plus the nucleocapsid protein. Joins with other viral proteins to form a complex capable of transcription and replication of nascent genomic RNA.

ribosomes—Small cytoplasmic particles that translate the information in mRNAs into proteins.

RNA—An abbreviation for ribonucleic acid. A long chain of ribonucleotides, usually single-stranded, that contains bases adenine, cytosine, guanine, and uracil. For some viruses, RNA contains the genetic information.

Glossary

spillover—Spillover infection is the occurrence of rabies with a particular endemic variant in another animal species. An example would be infection of skunks with a bat variant of rabies in an area known to be endemic for bat rabies.

substrate—The substance upon which an enzyme acts.

transcription—Synthesis of messenger RNA from a DNA or RNA template. The first step in gene expression.

transgenic plant—A plant, such as a tobacco plant, genetically engineered to contain a foreign gene from an unrelated organism (e.g., virus, animal, etc.).

translation—Process whereby the coding information in an mRNA directs the synthesis of a specific protein from amino acids.

trimers—A complex made up of three molecules of a monomer; for example, three G protein molecules complex to form a functional trimer.

vector—An organism or substance that can carry a gene or genes from another organism, and is used to deliver the foreign gene into a target host.

virion—A complete virus particle containing a DNA or RNA center with a protein coat and in some instances surrounded by an external envelope. This is the infective form of a virus.

virulence—The capacity of a virus to cause disease in a particular host.

virus—A microorganism smaller than bacteria, which cannot grow or reproduce outside of a living cell. Viruses enter cells and take over host cell functions to replicate themselves. The genetic material of viruses is either DNA or RNA. Rhinovirus is an example of a virus responsible for the common cold in humans.

wild type—A virus as found in nature (for example, rabies virus found in a raccoon).

xenotransplantation—Transplanting an organ from one species into another.

zoonoses (sing. zoonosis)—Diseases transmitted from a naturally infected animal host to humans.

zoonotic—Refers to the natural spread or transmission of a virus from an animal host to humans, such as spread of rabies from a dog to a human via a bite.

Bibliography

Bengis, R. G., F. A. Leighton, J. R. Fischer, M. Artois, et al. "The role of wildlife in emerging and re-emerging zoonoses." *Revue Scientifique et Technique {International Office of Epizootics}* 23 (2004): 497–511.

Belotto, A., L. F. Leanes, M. C. Schneider, H. Tamayo, and E. Correa. "Overview of rabies in the Americas." *Virus Research* 111 (2005): 5–12.

Belotto, A. J. "The Pan American Health Organization (PAHO) role in the control of rabies in Latin America." *Developmental Biology* (Basel) 119 (2004): 213–216.

Bleck, T. P., and C. E. Rupprecht. "Rhabdoviruses." In: *Clinical Virology*, 2nd edition, D. D. Richman, R. J. Whitley, and F. G. Hayden, eds. Washington, D.C.: ASM Press, 2002.

Cliquet, F., and M. Aubert. "Elimination of terrestrial rabies in Western European countries." *Developmental Biology* (Basel) 119 (2004): 185–204.

de Mattos, C. A., C. C. de Mattos, and C. E. Rupprecht. "Rhabdoviruses." In: *Fields Virology*, 4th ed., vol. 1, Philadelphia: Lippincott Williams & Wilkins, 2001.

Dietzschold, B., M. Faber, and M. J. Schnell. "New approaches to the prevention and eradication of rabies." *Expert Review of Vaccines* 2 (2003): 399–406.

Dietzschold, B., M. Schnell, and H. Koprowski. "Pathogenesis of rabies." *Current Topics in Microbiology and Immunology* 292 (2005): 45–56.

Ettinger, S. J., and E. C. Feldman. "Rabies Virus." In: *Textbook of Veterinary Internal Medicine, Diseases of the Dog and Cat*, 6th ed., vol. 1. St. Louis, Mo.: Elsevier Saunder, 2005.

Faber, M., R. Pulmanausahakul, K. Nagao, M. Prosniak, et al. "Identification of viral genomic elements responsible for rabies virus neuroinvasiveness." *Proceedings of the National Academy of Sciences, USA* 101 (2004): 16328–16332.

Finke, S., and K. K. Conzelmann. "Replication strategies of rabies virus." *Virus Research* 111 (2005): 120–131.

Fooks, A. R., S. M. Brooks, N. Johnson, L. M. McElhinney, and A. M. Hutson. "European bat lyssaviruses: an emerging zoonosis." *Epidemiology and Infection* 131 (2003): 1029–1039.

Hankins, D. G., and J. A. Rosekrans. "Overview, prevention, and treatment of rabies." *Mayo Clinic Proceedings* 79 (2004): 671–676.

Bibliography

Jayakar, H. R., E. Jeetendra, and M. A. Whitt. "Rhabdovirus assembly and budding." *Virus Research* 106 (2004): 117–132.

Knobel, D. L., S. Cleaveland, P. G. Coleman, E. M. Fèvre, et al. "Re-evaluating the burden of rabies in Africa and Asia." *Bulletin of the World Health Organization* 83 (2005): 360–368.

Lafon, M. "Rabies virus receptors." *Journal of Neurovirology* 11 (2005): 82–87.

Lafon, M. "Subversive neuroinvasive strategy of rabies virus." *Archives of Virology* Supplement 18 (2004): 149–159.

Lo Re III., V., and S. J. Gluckman. "Travel immunizations." *American Family Physician* 70 (2004): 89–99.

Mackenzie, J. S., and H. E. Field. "Emerging encephalitogenic viruses: lyssaviruses and henipaviruses transmitted by frugivorous bats." *Archives of Virology* Supplement (2004) (18): 97–111.

Maschke, M., O. Kastrup, M. Forsting, and H. C. Diener. "Update on neuroimaging in infectious central nervous system disease." *Current Opinion in Neurology* 17 (2004): 475–480.

Mayen, F. "Haematophagous bats in Brazil, their role in rabies transmission, impact on public health, livestock industry and alternatives to an indiscriminate reduction of bat population." *Journal of Veterinary Medicine. B Infectious Diseases and Veterinary Public Health* 50 (2003): 469–472.

McKenna, P. M., P. P. Aye, B. Dietzschold, D. C. Montefiori, et al. "Immunogenicity study of glycoprotein-deficient rabies virus expressing simian/human immunodeficiency virus $SHIV_{89.6P}$ envelope in a rhesus macaque." *Journal of Virology* 78 (2004): 13455–13459.

Murphy, F. A., E. P. J. Gibbs, M. C. Horzinek, and M. J. Studdert. "Rhabdoviridae." In: *Veterinary Virology*, 3rd edition. San Diego: Academic Press, 1999.

Pastoret, P. P., and A. Vanderplasschen. "Poxviruses as vaccine vectors." *Comparative Immunology, Microbiology and Infectious Disease* 26 (2003): 343–355.

Rose, J. K. and M. A. Whitt. "Rhabdoviridae: The Viruses and Their Replication." In: *Fields Virology*, 4th ed., vol. 1. Philadelphia: Lippincott Williams & Wilkins, 2001.

Rupprecht, C. E., C. A. Hanlon, and T. Hemachudha. "Rabies re-examined." *Lancet Infectious Diseases* 2 (2002): 327–343.

Schnell, M. J., G. S. Tan, and B. Dietzschold. "The application of reverse genetics technology in the study of rabies virus (RV) pathogenesis and for the development of novel RV vaccines." *Journal of Neurovirology* 11 (2005): 76–81.

Slate, D., C. E. Rupprecht, J. A. Rooney, D. Donovan, et al. "Status of oral rabies vaccination in wild carnivores in the United States." *Virus Research* 111 (2005): 68–76.

Taber, K. H., P. L. Strick, and R. A. Hurley. "Rabies and the cerebellum: new methods for tracing circuits in the brain." *Journal of Neuropsychiatry and Clinical Neurosciences* 17 (2005): 133–139.

Taplitz, R. A. "Managing bite wounds. Currently recommended antibiotics for treatment and prophylaxis." *Postgraduate Medicine* 116 (2004): 49–52, 55–56, 59.

Veterinary Medicine Today: Public Veterinary Medicine. "Compendium of animal rabies prevention and control, 2005." *Journal of the American Veterinary Medical Association* 226 (2005): 1304–1310.

Warrilow, D. "Australian bat lyssavirus: a recently discovered new rhabdovirus." *Current Topics in Microbiology and Immunology* 292 (2005): 25–44.

Wilde, H., P. Khawplod, T. Khamoltham, T. Hemachudha, et al. "Rabies control in South and Southeast Asia." *Vaccine* 23 (2005): 2284–2289.

Woldehiwet, Z. "Clinical laboratory advances in the detection of rabies virus." *Clinica Chimica Acta* 351 (2005): 49–63.

Wollman, G., P. Tattersall, and A. N. van den Pol. "Targeting human glioblastoma cells: comparison of nine viruses with oncolytic potential." *Journal of Virology* 79 (2005): 6005–6022.

World Health Organization Technical Report Series 931, First Report. WHO Expert Consultation on Rabies, World Health Organization, 2005 (Geneva, October 5–8, 2004).

Web Sites

All The Virology on the WWW
An excellent Web site for general information on viruses.
http://www.tulane.edu/~dmsander/garryfavweb.html

Bat Conservation International
For information on bats and the conservation of bats.
http://www.batcon.org/home/default.asp

Centers for Disease Control and Prevention
Comprehensive information on rabies.
http://www.cdc.gov/ncidod/dvrd/rabies/default.htm

Dog Owner's Guide to Rabies
http://www.canismajor.com/dog/rabies.html

General Cat Care
http://www.fanciers.com/cat-faqs/general-care.shtml

Global Atlas of infectious diseases
An interactive and information mapping system.
http://gamapserver.who.int/GlobalAtlas/home.asp

International Committee on Taxonomy of Viruses
Click on ICTVdB Index of Viruses, then enter rabies as search term.
http://www.ncbi.nlm.nih.gov/ICTVdb/Ictv/ICTVindex.htm

International Travel (HealthLink – Medical College of Wisconsin)
Information about pre-travel rabies vaccinations.
http://healthlink.mcw.edu/article/907109508.html

Kansas State University Rabies Lab
http://www.vet.ksu.edu/depts/rabies/

Pasteur Institute
Search for rabies on their home page.
http://www.pasteur.fr/english.html

RabAvert: Human Rabies Vaccine
http://www.rabavert.com

Traveler's Health Information from the Centers for Disease Control and Prevention
http://www2.ncid.cdc.gov/travel/yb/utils/ybGet.asp?section=dis&obj=rabies.htm

Wadsworth Center Rabies Laboratory
http://www.wadsworth.org/rabies/

World Health Organization
Human and animal rabies information.
http://www.who.int/rabies/en/

Index

acquired immune deficiency syndrome. *See* AIDS

acute neurologic syndrome, 27, 30, 34–35

adsorption, 22

Aedes aegypti, 19

Africa, 13, 63–65

agarose, 80–81

aggressiveness, 34, 37

agitation, 30, 37

AIDS (acquired immune deficiency syndrome), 6, 7, 63, 121

air, fear of, 34

Alabama, 50

Alaska, 51

American Society for Microbiology, 90

Angola, 65

anorexia, 30

anthrax, 10

antibodies, 37–38

antigens, 75

antiretroviral drugs, 7

anxiety, 30, 38

Argentina, 39

Aristotle, 8

Asia, 11, 13, 61–63

assembly process for new virions, 26

asymptomatic infection, 29

Australia, 67

Australian bat lyssavirus, 67

autonomic dysfunction, 30

baboon organ transplant, 33

Baby Fae, 33

Babylon, 8

Bacillus anthracis, 10

bacteria, 10, 19

badgers, 60

Bangladesh, 61

Barbados, 66

bats. *See also specific type of bat*

human rabies and, 45, 51–53, 56, 58, 60, 66, 98–101, 110–111, 112–114

in England, 67

Lago bat virus, 14, 65

post-exposure prophylaxis guide, 95

rabies reservoir, 13, 51

reported cases in, 49, 52, 59, 60, 61, 63

susceptibility to rabies, 9, 38, 39

beavers, 54, 95

Belgium, 66

big brown bat, 51

biting

cleaning, 86, 87

human exposure to, 58–59

spread of rabies by, 34

stage of rabies, 30, 37, 38, 40

blood-brain barrier, 27

Bolivia, 39

Botswana, 65

bovine viral diarrhea virus, 19

brain connections and rabies, 122–123

Brazilian free-tail bat, 51

Britain. *See* England

budding, 26

Buffy the Vampire Slayer, 102

cadaver, preservation of, 105–106

California, 50–51, 58

Canada, 48, 51, 59–60

cancer, targeting, 121

Caribbean islands, 39

carnivores, 95. *See also specific animal*

cats

in Africa, 65

post-exposure prophylaxis guide, 95

quarantine laws, 66, 67

reported cases in, 54, 55, 59, 60

seasonal trends, 56

susceptibility to rabies, 38, 39

vaccines, 11, 89, 92, 93, 94

cattle

reported cases in, 55, 57, 59

susceptibility to rabies, 14, 38

vaccines, 61, 92, 93

cDNA. *See* copy DNA

cell culture systems, 79

Celsus, Aulus Cornelius, 106

Centers for Disease Control, 48, 52, 90

Central America, 39

central nervous system. *See* CNS

Chain Reaction, 80

China, 8, 61, 62, 72, 106

Chlamydia, 17

cholera, 6

circoviruses, 19

classification of rabies virus biology, 14, 16

CNS (central nervous system), 27, 68, 71

cold sores, 29

coma, 27, 30, 35

condensation, 26

confusion, 34, 37

coordination, impaired, 34

copy DNA (cDNA), 80

corneal transplants, 32

cornea testing, 70–71

cotton rats, susceptibility to rabies, 38

cows, 10, 39, 111–112

coyotes

control programs, 44

rabies reservoir, 13

susceptibility to rabies, 38, 39

vaccines, 94

Crous, John M., 106

cryptosporidiosis, 6

cytology, 68

cytoplasm, 68

DDT, 6

dead-end host, 36

death

in Africa and Asia, 11, 13

in Australia, 67

Index

Index

About the Author

Thomas Kienzle, Ph.D., received a B.S. degree in Biology from Stockton State College in Pomona, New Jersey. He earned his doctorate from the University of Tennessee, Knoxville, TN. His doctoral research focused on characterization of the bovine coronavirus hemagglutinin protein gene. Also in graduate school, he taught General Biology as a teaching assistant. He completed postdoctoral training at the Baylor College of Medicine, Houston, Texas, on human herpes simplex virus type 1. His research was published in peer-reviewed journals as well as presented at scientific meetings. Dr. Kienzle is currently at the state veterinary diagnostic laboratory in Little Rock, AR, where he established a molecular diagnostics program for the detection of viral pathogens of animals. It is in this role that he comes into contact, on a daily basis, with tissues of animals that may be infected with many viruses, including the rabies virus.

About the Editor

The late **I. Edward Alcamo** was a Distinguished Teaching Professor of Microbiology at the State University of New York at Farmingdale. Alcamo studied biology at Iona College in New York and earned his M.S. and Ph.D. degrees in microbiology at St. John's University, also in New York. He had taught at Farmingdale for more than 30 years. In 2000, Alcamo won the Carski Award for Distinguished Teaching in Microbiology, the highest honor for microbiology teachers in the United States. He was a member of the American Society for Microbiology, the National Association of Biology teachers, and the American Medical Writers Association. Alcamo authored numerous books on the subjects of microbiology, AIDS, and DNA technology as well as the award-winning textbook *Fundamentals of Microbiology*, now in its sixth edition.